Lynne Tillman is the author of the novels *Haunted Houses*, *Motion Sickness*, *Cast in Doubt*, and *No Lease on Life*, and of two collections of short fiction, *Absence Makes the Heart* and *The Madame Realism Complex*. She wrote the text for *The Velvet Years: Warhol's Factory 1965–67* and was a co-editor of *Beyond Recognition: Representation, Power, Culture—Writings of Craig Owens*. Her criticism has appeared in *Art in America*, *Frieze*, *Artforum*, *Sight and Sound*, and the *Guardian*.

Other titles in this series

Gary Indiana
Let It Bleed

Steven Shaviro
Doom Patrols

Kathy Acker
Bodies of Work

Jonathan Romney
Short Orders

The Broad
Picture

essays

Lynne Tillman

Library of Congress Catalog Card Number: 96-71369

A catalogue record for this book is available from the British Library on request

The right of Lynne Tillman to be identified as the author of this work has been asserted by her in accordance with the Copyright, Designs and Patents Act 1988

All rights reserved under International and Pan-American Copyright Conventions

This collection copyright © 1997 by Lynne Tillman

[see copyright notices]

First published in 1997 by
Serpent's Tail, 4 Blackstock Mews, London N4
and 180 Varick Street, 10th floor, New York, NY 10014

Set in Sabon by Avon Dataset, Bidford-on-Avon
Printed in Great Britain by Mackays of Chatham

Copyright notice:

With the exception of "What Are Values?," "Like Rockets and Television II," Ugly," and "My Funny Ambivalence," the contents of this anthology were previously published in the following:

"Call It Local: *Specter of the Rose*," in *Picture This: Films Chosen by Artists*, ed. Steve Gallagher (Buffalo, N.Y.: Hallwalls, 1987).

"Love Story: Derek Jarman's *Caravaggio*," *Art in America* 75 (January 1987): 21–23.

"The Pleasure Principle," *Elle* (July 1989): 34–36.

"Thoroughly Modern Meals" [*The Futurist Cookbook*], *Voice Literary Supplement*, December 12, 1989, pp. 24–25.

"Slant" ["The Autobiography of Eve," on *A Mind of My Own* by Chris Costner Sizemore], *ArtForum* (April 1990): 24–27.

"The Real McCoy: *I Should Have Stayed Home*," *Voice Literary Supplement*, September 11, 1990, pp. 15–16.

"In Memoriam: Craig Owens," *Art in America* 78 (September 1990): 186.

"Where the Boy Is: *Ready to Catch Him Should He Fall* ["That's How Strong His Love Is"], *Voice Literary Supplement*, September 10, 1991, pp. 10–11.

"Critical Fiction/Critical Self," in *Critical Fictions: The Politics of Imaginative Writing*, ed. Philomena Mariani (Seattle: Bay Press, 1991), pp. 97–103.

"Hole Story," *Voice Literary Supplement*, February 1992, p. 12.

"Kiss of Death," *Sight and Sound* 2, no. 2 (June 1992): 33.

"Matisse: A Symposium," *Art in America* 81 (May 1993): 79–80.

"Looking for Trouble, or Privileging the Subtext," *Frieze* 12 (September–October 1993): 28–81.

"He Held It in His Hand Like a Leash" ["Penis Story"], *Guardian*, November 18, 1994, Living 4/5.

"An Impossible Man," in *Uncontrollable Bodies: Testimonies of Identity and Culture*, ed. Rodney Sappington and Tyler Stallings (Seattle: Bay Press, 1994).

"Boots and Remorse," in *Living with the Animals*, ed. Gary Indiana (London: Faber and Faber, 1994), pp. 187–201.

"Ray Charles," *Voice Literary Supplement*, April 1994, p. 11.

"Criminal Love," *Vogue* (Germany) (May 1995).

"Like Rockets and Television," in *The Velvet Years: Andy Warhol and the Factory 1965–1967* (London: Pavilion, 1995).

"Telling Tales," *Critical Quarterly* 37, no. 4 (Winter 1995).

"Past Shock," *Frieze*, Issue 29 (June–August 1996).

"My Funny Ambivalence in the Contact Zone," paper presented at "Negotiations in the Contact Zone, symposium organized by Renée Green, The Drawing Center, New York, April 9, 1994.

"Ugly," paper presented at "On Raciality and Literature," symposium organized by Cathy Taylor and Mosaic Books, St. Marks Poetry Project, New York, May 5, 1994.

"Like Rockets and Television II," paper presented at "Warhol's Worlds," conference organized by the Andy Warhol Museum, Pittsburgh, April 1995.

"What Are Values?," Spectacolor Big Board, Times Square, New York, 1987, project sponsored by the Public Art Fund.

Contents

Acknowledgments

I'd like to thank the editors, artists and curators, who suggested or commissioned these essays: Elizabeth C. Baker, Rona Berg, Louise Chunn, Pam Cook, Stacey D'Erasmo, Deborah Drier, Graham Fuller, Steve Gallagher, Renée Green, Gary Indiana, Colin MacCabe, Philomena Mariani, M. Mark, Nancy Marmer, Peter Nicholls, the Public Art Fund, Rodney Sappington and Tyler Stallings, Amanda Sharp, Stephen Shore, Matthew Slotover, Cathy Taylor, David Trinidad, and Brian Wallis.

My thanks to Amy Scholder for her gracious editorial help. To Ira Silverberg, who asked me to do this book, my sincerest gratitude.

I'd like to acknowledge with deepest appreciation two people who have, over the years, consistently and constructively aided the writing of these essays: Rosalyn Deutsche and Jane Weinstock.

And my special thanks to David Hofstra, for his steady rhythm and relentless, ironic humor, and for his being in time with me.

For Andrew Hill and Rebecca Hill

Preface: Mirrors
and Screens

One day I'd like to produce a jigsaw puzzle called The Grassy Knoll. It would be made of a million pieces and include every conspiracy theory about JFK's assassination in Dallas. Every theory, every player, would have a place. Some theories would conflict with others—most—but they'd be on the board. Even if it could be put together, it would negate parts of itself. (It would be easier to do virtually.) I was telling some friends about it at an outdoor party. We were sitting on a grassy knoll. I laughed and said: The puzzle would be as big as the grassy knoll itself.

Writing allows for the little and big pieces of people's lives and thoughts, coming out of a multitude of conditions, attitudes, moods, positions. Essays are like mirrors and screens, decorated with reflections and projections. These pieces (I'll give you a piece of my mind) sample a broad range of subjects, mental states, ideas, from crime and death to memory and forgetting, from art, books and movies to psychoanalysis, from fascism to feminism, from victims and mad love to narrative, from Warhol's place in these disunited states to hometown racism. What fascinates, horrifies and obsesses me pops up at different moments and in different guises. The guises are in the first person and third person, in the subjective and objective voices, sometimes within the same piece. There are shifts. I shift, things shift, I shift with them or don't.

Various as they are (Gary Indiana told me they were), together these essays might comprise a catalogue or menu of cultural objects. The relationship of "them" and "me" is an arranged marriage; and no divorce is possible. To paraphrase Goebbels who was quoted by Godard: When I hear the word "culture," I reach for myself.

Uncertainties (as well as assholes) rule at the end of the so-called American Century. The search for "lasting values" is a stand-up comic's implicit source of jokes, and lasting values, or the desire for immortality, may be the next old/new frontier—infinitely unreachable. Evidence of success or failure or anything else has become, in the wake of O.J., as indeterminate as the crack in The Golden Bowl. Who could say now, "It fits like a glove." Who can say what's fit or what really fits. It was hard choosing these essays, the right fit for this book. (Including and excluding are the blessings and curses of choice in a democracy.)

Ideas are only human. I worry about slavish devotion to any idea or principle, since if ideas, beliefs, and principles are raised to the power of Truth, righteousness soon follows, and all hope is lost. I have questions and doubts. Questions can be less partial than answers to them.

Concocting this preface is a little like doing the makeup for a face, which will appear on the head of a body of work. So I've decided to consider this face mental space. Mental space is maybe all I really have, it's maybe what an essay is, and to the extent that I have it, I've tried to use it.

Lynne Tillman
September 1996

1. An Impossible Man

Daddy's lying on the floor, on his back. I'm sitting on his chest—I'm two or younger. I sit very close to his face. I kiss his face all over. I love him before reason.

There's a sense, it's longing, probably, that I could join, if there was enough time, all the time of the world, that tiny moment with the present—if something like that would occur in infinity—and feel his skin, his face, the face I touched then.

He touched me and left unquestioned and questionable marks on me. I couldn't control my strangest, happiest, darkest, wildest, and most unsettled responses to him, with him. He was almost a response in me; he occupied not just a part of me, not just a place in my life, but life, in the beginning. At the very least he was there at the beginning.

"In the beginning" signals the start of unresolved and unresolvable stories. In the beginning is fantasy, Freud's "protective fiction," and the fantastic is beautiful and horrible. Fantasy is one of the tenacious claims of childhood.

(I have a memory of him, but it's not him. It's my will-him-into-being. He's a lost and a found object.)

My father died ten years ago. I didn't believe he would, I just mouthed the words. Then he did. It seems simpler, easier to write about dead people. They can't object, or complain, and as far as stories go, there's a "natural" and "appropriate" ending to appropriate for one's own ends. But it's harder, really, because of one's compulsion, need to, which is inhibited and chastened by the lack of the object who could object. There isn't a yearning to write about the living as if they were alive; they are. Even friends or enemies who have merely fallen away are still alive and have the potential for presence again. Bad things can be undone, maybe. There's no potential from death. Except, a common wisdom goes, for the living to expect freedom, a kind of deserved liberation. It's reassuring and handy, as if "freedom" were death's dowry. When really it's incommensurability.

My father was one of three boys, sons. He was the middle son, his mother's favorite. He became the father to three girls, daughters. (I'm the youngest.) He was, I thought as a child, sometimes uncomfortable, or awkward, in our family: he was the only man at the dinner table, the only man on our trips, the only man at our table in a restaurant. We shared him, unequally, it would turn out. Each daughter had a different father, her own father, and the mother/wife, a husband who was different from the father. (I didn't realize that, then.)

My father was special especially in his difference from us. His singularity was a kind of burden to him, I think. An insecure man, he was uncertain about how to be with girls and vulnerable because of his uncertainty. At least he seemed to me, when I was little, vulnerable because of it. I grew up believing that he was—and consequently men were—as sensitive as we were. Maybe more.

I can remember thinking that my father's having his penis on the outside of his body was another sign of his vulnerability, his fragility. We girls were so much more compact and lucky, I thought. Our sex was protected.

One afternoon my father was about to sit down on a couch in the den.

Lynne (age eight or nine): Aren't you afraid you're going to break it?

Daddy: What?

Lynne: Your penis.

Daddy: Why?

Lynne: Don't you have bones in it?

Daddy: In my penis? No. Who told you that?

Lynne: I learned the word "boner" at school. You don't have bones in it?

Daddy collapses on the couch, laughing.

But Daddy's penis was no laughing matter. It was never mentioned. He had to "cover himself," to guard us from his nakedness when we reached a certain age, but since I was the youngest, while he and my sisters were already covering themselves in front of each other, I could still be uncovered and so could he. I went to the toilet with him and watched him piss. I took my first shower with him because, at the age of five, I was afraid of showers. He said he'd take me in with him, and he'd bring an umbrella. We got in, and he slid the glass doors shut. He opened the umbrella and turned the water on. We stood there, not getting wet. Then, when I wasn't anxious anymore, he closed the umbrella. I don't remember talking about it again. Maybe it was our secret. More likely he and my mother laughed about it later, privately.

He loved to laugh, but he often appeared surprised to find something funny. His eyebrows—maybe one more than the other— would jump up onto his forehead, as if he were puzzled or curious that something could make him laugh, and then, having thought it over, he'd laugh. But my father was given as much—more—to depression. He careened from high to low, where he stayed longer, all his fortunate and unfortunate life. He could be petulant, childish, and demanding; he had his way more often than not. He seemed to need to be taken care of.

("In human beings," Freud wrote, "pure masculinity or femininity is not to be found either in a psychological or a biological sense." Early on I saw my father as vulnerable and my mother as tough, very tough, tougher than she really was, especially in relation to him, I learned later.)

He seemed to need to be taken care of, though he was physically strong. Until my father had his first heart attack, I had never seen him sick. Sometimes he stuck pieces of Dr. Scholl's rubber pads between two of his toes, which crossed. Maybe I was aware that he slept badly. But that, to me, wasn't being sick, then. His illness was intangible, irrational—anxiety, depression, guilt. Neurosis. It was the valley I entered when I walked downstairs to the basement to sit next to him, to try to make him feel better.

November 1990

Dream that my sister B. tells me—she wakes me up in my dream to tell me—that Daddy's had another heart attack, and part of his heart, a greater part of his heart, is atrophied. He's not dead? I ask. No, she says. And then Daddy and Uncle J. walk into her former apartment. Maybe—I'm not sure—there's a hallway. Daddy's kind of sheepish, almost embarrassed at being alive. It's an expression I remember him having when he felt I loved him too much. I throw my arms around him and say, I'm so glad you're not dead.

His beginnings were meager, poor. He was a first-generation American, with an immigrant Russian Jewish mother and father; his father was a shirt maker. I don't know what my father felt about his father. His father didn't live with them but visited weekly; it's a story I never learned enough about. My mother says his family was never hungry. None of his brothers is alive to ask about the early days. I have no idea what their apartment looked like. If I were a visitor in my father's house—maybe I am—it would be strange to me. I don't know how I found out he was his mother's favorite. Maybe my mother told me, or his brother, or he did, long ago.

One night, when he was married, in his own apartment and already a father, he was eating a delicious steak. Excited, he woke my sisters—I wasn't born yet—because he wanted them to have a taste. I can imagine the scene: Daddy sitting close to his little daughters on their beds, their eyes half shut with sleep. He is eagerly, happily, feeding them pieces of what money can buy.

He loved to eat. He used to exclaim that I was so delicious he was going to put me in the oven, cook me, and eat me. I was confused about that, because he loved food, so it was a compliment, to be wanted like that. But I didn't want to be cooked in the oven, that was terrifying. But just as now I can't separate his psychical body from his physical body, as a child—and maybe for children generally—there was no way to make a distinction, to divorce absolutely the pleasure of his wanting to eat me from not wanting to be put in the oven. Everything was possible, impossibly real, and make-believe.

(If my father had been a writer, perhaps he would've concocted a fairy tale about a father who loves his children so much he wants to eat them. I probably am.)

Writing, I catch traces of his hands in mine, they sneak up through my fingers as particles, the short, light hairs above my knuckles, part of my inheritance from him. I have short hands, too, or small hands. Actually, my hands are more like my mother's.

My father's hands are gripping the steering wheel, and he's driving me into the city, New York, and he and I are alone.

Lynne (nine): Manhattan is an island?

Daddy: Yes.

We are crossing the 59th Street Bridge, and I looked ahead at the huge buildings on the island.

Lynne: Why doesn't it just sink?

He glanced at me, bemused or dubious, I'll never know. I wanted to interest him. He explained what an island was, that Manhattan wouldn't sink just like that, fast. I believed, maybe mistakenly, that he enjoyed the ridiculous idea, the absurdity, that it might sink, just like that.

(Maybe he fought all his life against seeing himself as ridiculous and was at home with the absurd and could play ridiculously with me.)

I wasn't satisfied with his island answer, whatever it actually was. I didn't have a strong sense of the physical world. I wanted it to be there and not to be a problem. I wanted it to be a stable foundation, but it wasn't a foundation for me, really.

(Is the body a foundation, and for what?)

My father liked driving, to jump behind the wheel and go. Let's go to Coney Island. Let's go to town and pick up a pint of coffee ice cream. Let's go to the docks and look at the boats. Except there were terrible fights in the car, and my mother would scream that he pull over because otherwise we'd have an accident. He could turn, in an instant, from a charming Dr. Jekyll into a snarling Mr. Hyde.

June 1992

Dream I am in a strange house, with D., who's not there, and P., who tells an advertising exec, an old man, to call and see me. I give him directions to the house, but can't remember the street I'm on, a cross-section with some French names or phrases, familiar ones I can't remember now. The earlier part of the dream was horrific—a man stuffed himself inside a large, bearlike dog and then committed suicide; the last shot of him was with a maniacal but dead grin on his face, his eyes wide open. I think P. gives me and the old man a ride, or just me, to go visit the old man. P. drives like a maniac.

Daddy could become a monster on purpose. When my friends came to the house, he played this game—Want me to scare you? We'd sit in the dark den, happy fear building as minutes passed, waiting for my father to throw open a door—we never knew which one or when—and charge in, like the creature from the Black Lagoon. He'd creep slowly toward us, all misshapen and bent over, then stand over us, waving his arms like a lunatic, and leap up and down, making weird noises, being the bogeyman. Sometimes he did that when I was alone in my bed upstairs. It was, definitionally, thrilling. He was my prohibited, purloined father/lover, a monstrous desire, appropriately in gothic drag.

*

(But for him? What did it serve? Did it relieve him of the burden of being a monster the times when it wasn't on purpose, when he couldn't control himself?)

The longer he's dead, the harder it is for me to remember in any detail or with any vividness how he forced me, bodily, out the front door of the house; how he chased me around the house with a strap; how I hid from him in the bathroom and locked the door. When I try to call up scenes like these, to set them on the stage of memory, or to stage them as memory, a dull curtain descends. The scene meets interference, is somehow obliterated or forced off. And the memory withers, frays, as if it can't hold up to scrutiny or can't be contained, not the thought of it. Then I—who am I then?— fumble to replace the bad lost moment with a less terrible but no less lost moment. And it's then that I'm most aware of picking and choosing a past, a father.

Probably the people who are most afraid make and become the best monsters; it must be a counterphobic truism. My father was preyed upon by his fears. He often quoted "the only thing we have to fear is fear itself," and he feared it, the unnameable. As a child he was terrified by the rats in the basement where he was sent to collect coal. Maybe he was afraid of the older, tougher neighborhood boys, the loss of his mother's love, his older brother's anger. The alien world outside his immigrant mother's apartment.

There were two stories he told me about job hunting. One time he was advised that the way to find a job was: Go to a very tall office building, to the top, and then walk down every floor, and knock on every door, asking if anyone needs help. He followed that advice. The other story was about the first job he actually applied for, when he was twelve. He wanted to be a busboy. He thought busboys worked on buses, and he'd spend his summer vacation seeing America. Instead he carried trays.

He was comforting about my fears of the shower, of dying when I was six, of not being able to "do the work" in first grade. After watching an educational movie at school, when I was seven, that showed how kids playing on the Long Island Railroad's third rail were electrocuted and how a little girl was blinded because bad boys threw stones at the windows of the train, I feared the Long Island Railroad. I didn't want to go anywhere on a train ever again. One day my father took me to the city by train. When the train crossed over a trestle, where bad boys could've waited as they did in the educational movie, I dropped to the floor. If my father tried to reassure me, which I don't remember, he didn't insist I sit in my seat immediately or pressure me to get off the floor. He acknowledged my terror, took it to heart, or at least respected my anxiety, or knew how improbable it was that he could change my mind about fear.

If he feared the loss of his mother's love, he never hated her. If he feared the loss of her love, then all his life he took care of her, generously, without complaint. I thought, as a child, he was even proud of her, though she was strange, different, difficult—foreign. He provided her with her own comfortable apartment, with a nurse or housekeeper when she needed it. He dressed her in fur coats when, my mother still remarks, she herself wore a cloth coat.

August 1990
Dream that Daddy is dying again. I see him alive, with his face very full, like his mother's. But then he turns into my mother, and she is dying. Then I am given a copy of Ronald Fraser's *In Search of the Past*, a book which I had already bought for myself.

Actually, I keep forgetting his face, it's blurred as if my glasses were permanently lost. Going away, gone now, there now, *fort/da*. He's transparent, an empty illusion. His nails—I don't see them. They were wide, stubby maybe, hard, not easily broken. I can vaguely visualize his arms—they were well formed. So were his legs. And though his chest had almost no hair on it, his forearms were covered with dark-brown hair. Descriptive words come easily, but not him; words for loss, too, though there aren't enough of them, and they're inadequate, because none is sufficient for how nothing it all is. None is as absent as absence. Already in his ephemeral image is death, and he's never a solid body anymore.

(If I write "I hold an image of him," the image dissipates faster than those words can be read. But you can return to the words.)

When my father wrote letters, he usually wrote over some of his words, to correct his penmanship, to make each letter clearer. The result was a sloppiness I interpreted as playfulness, impatience, or frustration—some kind of inventiveness. Trying to find his hand, I sometimes imitate his handwriting. I trace over the letters of words though they can be read. I could stop myself, but I don't want to. There's a second of indecision, and I know if I do it, the letter will become sloppy, but I do it anyway, as if to say, it's out of my control, can't be helped. I'm my father's daughter. It's feeble—this attempt to exhume him, to find him in me as if I were the ground or surface and he were a deeper layer. I feel something when I do it, but it's false, too deliberate.

When he was a kid, my father played a lot of handball (he saved the leather glove that he used to wear on his right hand), and he could play much later in life. He wasn't as good at tennis as my mother, he was strong and wild; but on the handball court, he was fast and accurate. And he was short—my father used to joke that he would be a star basketball player in a midget league—but he was proud of his well-developed body, and aware that he was handsome. He liked to stay fit and, way before jogging was fashionable, he would take us girls for runs with him on the beach, in the winter, to develop our leg muscles. He would always insist that we hold ourselves erect, backs straight—Stomachs In!—and one exercise he had us do was: Stand against a wall and descend into a squatting position, then sit there, to strengthen thigh and stomach muscles, then shimmy up, keeping spines flat against the wall. (To this day posture is important to me. Backbone?)

He didn't have sons, he was athletic. (Not surprisingly, as the last, late child, I was supposed to be the boy.) He conducted exercises with us as if we were in the army—he was the sergeant. It was always a little funny; he thought it was funny too, I think, or maybe ridiculous and ironic. Here we were being his sons in a kind of masquerade of "masculinity."

(Could I have learned to appreciate "masculinity as masquerade"? Do I now?)

He was a textile converter, a designer of fabrics, and an innovator of synthetic threads. Though he was one of the bosses, he chose for his office a very small room, a large closet; his beloved baby brother (by fifteen months), Al, his partner, took the grand "executive" room. My father thought Al was "the creative one." He deferred to his baby brother, who died much earlier than he.

Uncle Al's was the first dead body I ever saw, lying in a coffin, in a plain room of bereavement. My father and his uncle, for whom Al was named, stood at the casket. My great-uncle was at Al's foot, crying, my father near Al's head, staring at his face. He was waiting for Al to come alive. Hopelessness, anguish, despair, a longing I'd never known, drew his face into a portrait of intolerable sadness. I had never seen him look that way before (or ever again, it would turn out). Where he could not forgive himself, or us, anything, Daddy could always forgive Al.

December 1990
Dream Daddy's alive, but then he dies. I say to my mother, At least I got to hear his voice again.

I couldn't believe Pop—that's how he signed his letters and how he was addressed by us sometimes—would die. He was supposed to have died four years before he did. The doctors called his being alive "a miracle." They didn't explain what that meant until he did die. Then we were told that my father had only 18 percent of his heart muscle working; the rest was atrophied. The miracle was that people are not supposed to be able to survive with less than 33 percent of their heart functioning.

He read everything about the heart and had his own theories. One was to exercise, no matter what. The other was to have a teaspoon of cider vinegar every day, "to cut the grease." He had low cholesterol, so he told us that the hardening of his arteries was genetic, not environmental, and cholesterol didn't always matter. He kept up his strength. He used to go for fast walks, with weights around his ankles. He wanted to build up his heart. In part, the doctors attributed the miracle to the fact that all his other organs were in good condition. He was strong. There was nothing wrong with him except his bum heart, we all said.

January 1992

Dream that, after visiting W.'s house, whose wine glasses are sparkling clean, spotless, I'm in a small kitchen. There is a bottle of dishwashing liquid. It's pink. It's called Miracle.

The night he nearly died, my two sisters, my mother, and I waited in the hospital waiting room, all night. Four women, all for him. Pop was never easy in his harem; he was embarrassed, perhaps, at his largesse, the excessiveness, the display of females around him. But he was also vain. Probably we fed his pride while simultaneously humiliating him. He was easily humiliated and wanted to be liked. The only man in our family, he was privileged to be unique in our midst. And to be depressed, generous, moody, inquisitive (he read late at night, books scattered all over the floor around his side of the bed), surly, playful, violent, angry, weak, handsome, smart, harebrained. All these things. A man, the only one. He was allowed a wide range, a wide berth, by me.

(My father must have represented to me a mix of "feminine" and "masculine" attributes, a balance, unbalanced, in one body. I see how I align him with his "active" body, the physical house for a sometimes "passive" man. But what is "active" and what is "passive"? Aren't these terms as unfixed and unstable as sexuality itself?)

Death destabilizes and unfixes. I look at photographs of Pop. He's different in each. Death deconstructs. Daddy's unstable and unfixed. A picture is always a picture. Inevitably, each one disappoints, it's a flimsy post-factum. Just a picture I like or don't. I keep mental images.

His upper lip was fuller than his bottom one, which I can't recall at all, and one side of his upper lip was raised more than the other, but I can't remember which side. Facing him, I think it would be his left side. His eyes were large and hazel, sometimes nearly green. To me he looked like Gene Kelly and the aged Henry Fonda of *On Golden Pond* and the top of John Garfield's head, from the eyes up, and the bottom of the older James Mason's face, the line of his mouth especially. And an elderly Chinese man I once passed on Mott Street. The Chinese man had deep creases in his face, which my father didn't ever have, but he looked uncannily like my father. I catch flashes of him in countless other men and women, and infants—he's a shake of the head, an innocuous movement, a flared nostril. I'll see him for a second in mental pictures as various and inconclusive as photographs. He's buried in many places.

His mother told him he was born on the Fourth of July, so he was an American baby. His birthday was a minor family mystery. He found out he was born on June 28, and for a while that's when we celebrated it. Then, he discovered, but I don't know how, maybe he finally dug out his birth certificate, that he was born on June 29. Right now I remember that for years he thought my birthday was the day after it is. He was never sure. I thought it was funny.

July 1992

Dream that my father has lost a tooth in the back of his mouth. There's a gaping hole in his gum, and it's bleeding. He is indifferent and seems not at all to care. In fact, he is buoyant and energetic, even happy and excited. He is not dead, as he usually is in my dreams. I'm living in a dismal, shabby apartment. A light fixture is damaged; I ask the landlady to repair it. But she says it's not her job. I say, I thought furnished apartments had to be taken care of by the owners. She says no. I walk around the apartment and discover a room that would be perfect for me to write in, and I feel happier about the place. But it's part of someone else's apartment, which I just enter. They're eating dinner, a big family sitting around a large table. They're not unfriendly, but they are surprised.

*

I accept some of the picture my father had of himself. Even if it's unclear or out of focus, in it he's in the body he liked. He's never just an idea, a thing, an abstraction, though he is by now the most absolute and resolute of abstractions, horribly abstract, in pieces, and undeniably and palpably only symbolic.

(Part of loving, maybe, is to love someone as he or she wants to be loved. I don't know. I can't make a decision about how to love him.)

When I was ten, I knew my father was aware of my body. My mother, father, and I had just been to my father's office, and we were crossing 42nd Street. I was walking ahead of my parents. A man bumped or knocked into me. I kept walking. But my father grabbed the man. He looked as if he was about to hit him, and shouted: I saw what you did. I could call the cops. I saw you. My father's rage, so often directed at us, turned on the stranger, a man. I'm not sure what happened next. I think my father glared at the man as he rushed away. My father stood there. (Should I write "impotently"? He may have experienced a lack in the language that defines and constructs lack for men, a diminution of "manly" power.) He wanted to murder the man who had felt up his pubescent daughter. And he must have known how incapable he was of stopping assaults on me by other men. I think I was aware of that then. My mother and I waited on the sidewalk and watched him as he continued to stand there. He was in the valley again. Then we walked on in silence. What had occurred was unspeakable. Though I was supposed to be the injured party, I wasn't taken care of. My narcissistic father, in a sense, suffered the greater blow, which I witnessed. It troubled me more than the man hitting against me. I was ignorant of what he was doing. If my father hadn't erupted, I wouldn't have known. I knew my father was hurt.

My father's most pungent advice about men was: "Don't be the omnipotent female and think you can change a man. You can't." My mother was always trying to change him, he thought. She couldn't, of course. He didn't hand out much advice about men. I don't think he really knew what to say to us about them, was too self-conscious, being one himself. (Dirty jokes bothered him, and he never told them. Was it because he had daughters or a strange, prohibiting, beloved mother?) I didn't talk to him about my boyfriends, anyway. But one time, when I was grown up, I received a letter from a man I was involved with, a poet. Paying attention to form, the poet wrote the sentences in circles, and to read the letter, I had to turn the paper around and around. My father watched as I read it. Finally, when I had finished, he said, almost indifferently: I'm glad I don't know people like that.

Even so, I prevailed upon him to give me something, a present, to offer to the poet, my erstwhile lover. Sheepishly, my father gave me a Cuban cigar. I could tell it was another ironic gesture.

(Is my father a delusion I shared with him? Was it shared?)

I suppose, though, the ironic gesture I remember most was more sustained, a trope of "masculinity" rather than a single gesture. It was my father's being the sole financial support of the family until his business began to do poorly, and my mother took a part-time job (by then I was fifteen or sixteen). If there was something about the traditional expectations set for men, about what men were supposed to do, that made them—my father—most vulnerable in my eyes, it was this: supporting the family. I studied my anxious father. He worried constantly, putting money in the stock market one day, taking it out the next. He wasn't much of a capitalist. (I think it's why I appreciate *Death of a Salesman*. It can be read as much for "the problems men face" as for "the problems men face under capitalism.")

January 1994

Dream my father dies, and I start to cry. My mother says: But you sat on his lap for two hours before he died.

I write and sit on his lap. I have my father, at least for two hours. Writing about him, I play with him, his body. Since he's dead, he can't object as I know he would if he were alive. But then I wouldn't write this if he were alive. He would hate it. Or he wouldn't countenance it. He'd turn his face away. My unabashed love for him was weird to him, but he acknowledged it. Two years before he died, he and my mother presented me with a framed photograph of him when he was five years old, taken by a photographer who traveled around on horseback. It's hand-tinted.

(What if he didn't love me? What if every interpretation I make is wrong? Is his love for me my necessary illusion? Questions and doubts propose their own resonant and inadequate "answers." When he was alive, his devastating tantrums and violence were a kind of natural disaster. We had a tempestuous relationship. We got along better on the telephone. But I can't relinquish a mostly flattering picture of him. Should I?)

Daddy dead is as unwieldy and vague and unpredictable and resilient and unsure as he was alive.

He loved the ocean.

He dived under big waves, swam far out, and did laps.

He liked to watch the owls in the baseball stadium in Florida, so he went to night games.

He was a graceful dancer.

He fed fish in the artificial pond behind his apartment.

He cooked leftovers with soy sauce, but most of it was inedible.

He clipped articles from the newspaper, showed them to me or mailed them to me.

He always had a lot of change, which he placed on top of his chest of drawers.

His drawers were messy.

He made faces.

He liked to pull out crabgrass from the lawn.

He had good eyesight and only late in life did he need reading glasses, which he wore at the end of his nose.

He liked to nap after he ate.

He played gin every Tuesday night with four men who called

him "The Pelican," because he'd finish their food.

He became violently seasick on boats.

He fell asleep at the opera, when he and my mother had season tickets.

He hated sex scenes in movies and didn't like most movies, especially toward the end of his life.

He loved salty food.

He liked to lecture.

He smoked cigars and pipes.

He was proud that his business had a good rating from Dun and Bradstreet.

He hated Mick Jagger.

He read books to find answers.

He prepared his taxes by himself.

He knew the words to one song only, his high school's: "We are the Boys of Boys High," which he sang flat.

(My mother has a good singing voice. And she loves movies. She sees everything, usually by herself. She even saw *The Silence of the Lambs* alone. When I was a kid, I watched movies on TV with her a lot, and when she dies, though it's impossible and I don't believe it, I'll go to the movies without her. Movies could become my imaginary mother. And that will be another story. Then I'll remember how my not-so-very-tough mother looked when she asked, probably rhetorically, at the end of a movie on TV: Lynne, what are you crying about? She says my father was not an unhappy man.)

I could go on. It's futile. Writing emerges from it and records it, I think, and the desire to set it down, get it out, get it down, put it out, him, his stuff and mine, makes any writerly desire comic, converts a page turner into a stomach turner. It turns my stomach. But then it is also absolutely what I want to do.

Without my consent and with it, totally, I'm driven to mark things out of a life that will end against its will. It's a death I can't write. Uncontrollable death is at the center, central to meaning, central to meaninglessness. Texts will be read in different ways at different times, to mean different things, if they're read at all. They're lively, living bodies. Or dead bodies. Like Daddy who's gone.

Nathan Tillman   June 29, 1908—August 7, 1984

1994

2. Critical Fiction/ Critical Self

Perhaps it is in this project of learning how to represent *ourselves*—how to speak *to*, rather than for or about, others—that the possibility of a "global" culture resides.

—Craig Owens, *Art in America* (July 1989)

What I keep telling myself is that I want to make this simple, to make things simple; I want to be direct. I want to say why I write and what I write for, and out of, in as clear a way as possible—to cut to the chase or to the quick, to get to the heart of it. But nothing seems simple and I'm not certain why I write or in whose name other than my own, which is not really my name, but my father's, which is a made-up Ellis Island name, anyway.

To be able to make things simple I'd have to think that I was in control of myself, my language, my situation, my world. I'm not; I'm also not completely out of control. I write out of language, out of my world, out of myself, but I am not on top of the world and on top of the language that makes up the world and which makes me up, as I try desperately to make up other worlds. This essay is, in a way, for me, another world, one that I am now asking you to enter, which already seems a certain kind of demand. It has been hard for me, psychologically, and as a woman, to make demands, to negotiate a space from which I can demand—writing is a demand to be read and heard—and consequently it has been hard for me to become a writer.

I choose to write—fiction primarily, though I write nonfiction, too—because, especially lately, it gives me pleasure, though why that came about I'm not sure. I do know I decided to become a writer when I was eight and that I stuck to the idea; I held the notion deep inside me, for me alone and for a long time. I think it sustained me or gave me a me to sustain. What kind of decision could it have been then and even now? I need to write, I think, but need is an odd thing. I need to in the sense that writing gives me an identity, a thing to be in the world, gives me something to do, and so on. I never want to forget or diminish my own pleasure and narcissism, for while I may insist that I write fiction critically and not just for myself, it is also critical for me—whoever I am (I wish all my I's could be in quotes)—to write.

I hope this beginning doesn't put you off. Beginnings are difficult; in the beginning one must immediately impose a direction from which a character, a statement, a mood, or a frame of reference will be established or determined. And, most important, a voice, the ineffable voice. My unease—dis-ease—at discussing my writing of "critical fiction" is central to how I write, in any case. And one of the reasons I choose to write fiction is that just this kind of ambiguity and ambivalence can find its way into a story or into that complex cultural unit called a novel, where, as Bakhtin put it, a "struggle between one's own and another's word is being waged," and which represents the world as a multiplicity of voices, as heteroglossia.

It reassures me that Bakhtin thinks this, by the way; it is one of the theories I look to for sustenance and support when I feel that what I am engaged in is futile, that the forces I am or imagine myself fighting are so much bigger, so much more powerful that it's all hopeless. I know this is not a good attitude. I also take solace in sayings like Pessimism of the Intellect, Optimism of the

Will. I look to many theories—psychoanalytic, literary, feminist, art, Marxist, sociological, film, cultural theories of all kinds—for help, for succor, for explanations and amplifications; they are heuristic tools with which to dig up, and into, the world.

If I assert I write fiction critically, I must set out what it is I oppose and am critical of, but I am dubious about asserting this, and so simultaneously—in a superimposition or as a split-screen image—wish to impose the question whether or not I can actually achieve this: a position of difference, writing differently, thinking differently, reading differently. All of these activities are related, requiring that others be captured by—and captive to—the same project and spirit. Whatever independent thinking is, if it is, it happens dependently; it depends on others, on the life of minds which, like one's own, are socially—nationally and internationally, if you will—and psychologically constructed. One is not entirely alone in being alone with one's thoughts. So the writing of critical fiction takes place within communities, some of which may not recognize themselves as such but in the act of writing and reading differently become known to themselves.

I am wary or shy of proposing my fiction as written in opposition to, or to pronounce that I write differently, as if I—or it—could transcend conditions of birth and development—its and mine—and was somehow able to escape them. Or even that I knew, and the writing could locate, the right problems. It's certainly on my agenda—to challenge the complacent, to question national, familial, racial, and sexual arrangements, to resist structures and institutions that serve the powerful and perpetuate powerlessness. But as I wrote of the narrator in my novel *Motion Sickness*—an American moving from place to place in foreign lands—"I must contribute daily, involuntarily, but in small and big ways toward keeping the world the way it is." (The question of agency haunts the novel.)

I'm struggling to find a way to think about all this, to be articulate and write something meaningful, which is supposed to be a writer's job. Anton Shammas speaks of himself as a "Third World" person, a Palestinian citizen of Israel writing in Hebrew, who is "un-Jewing the Hebrew language," "undoing the culture of the majority from within." He quotes Gilles Deleuze and Félix Guattari's work on Kafka and minor literature—"that which a minority constructs within a major language." Deleuze and Guattari work to empty the minor—the marginal—of unimportance. "There is nothing that is major or revolutionary except the minor." And I take heart from "it is literature that produces an active solidarity in spite of skepticism."

> If one is a woman one is often surprised by a sudden splitting off of consciousness, say in walking down Whitehall, when from being the natural inheritor of that civilisation, she becomes, on the contrary, outside of it, alien and critical.
> —Virginia Woolf, *A Room of One's Own*

I'm not claiming to be a Kafka, to write a dialect, or to be inventing a new language; I work within the American English language as a white, middle-class, second-generation American woman, at a particular moment in history, with my own particular biography. (Sometimes, like now, looking at the categories into which I fit, writing myself like this, I am, frankly, stultified.) So I must wrest this language and its forms away from or out of "the majority" (of which I am a part, in some ways and at some times, to others), to un-man it, to un-American it, even to un-white it, to inconvenience the majority language, to unconventionalize it, even to shame it, in an odd sort of way, to question privilege, my own, too, of course. (While I don't have to un-man myself—maybe de-man myself and my writing—perhaps in the process of writing I may be able to approach un-Americaning and un-whiting myself.)

It seems odd—haughty (bad girl)—to write of un-manning language or un-Americaning it, especially un-whiting it, as if I could. Still when I sat down to write *Haunted Houses* (I remember being taught that Hemingway stood, as if that made him heroic and construed writing itself as virile activity), the challenge was to make unfamiliar the lives of girls in a language that is often hostile to "girls," that has a history of being hostile to girls and women. To construct "girls" in fiction, to represent them in writing, seemed to require a kind of wrestling match with an unwilling opponent. It was the case of writing against what I took to be the way women and girls were usually written. In fact the project was to take seriously female narratives, which often aren't, from masturbation fantasies to female friendship to girls studying philosophy to women writing, and to make the writing of those narratives, the writing itself, the subject of the book as well. All the time, I was engaged with and writing to and against an invisible, implacable but indifferent enemy—I was no threat—and sometimes what it was I was against—up against—was beyond my comprehension, or so far inside me that I could never find it. In a way, too, I was just writing, and writing itself was sufficient for me.

> One goes into the room—but the resources of the English language would be much put to the stretch, and whole flights of words would need to wing their way illegitimately into existence before a woman could say what happens when she goes into a room.
>
> —Virginia Woolf, *A Room of One's Own*

"Whole flights of words would need to wing their way illegitimately" astonishes me—how accurate Woolf is about the unspeakable, the inadmissible, what cannot be said or has not been written. My emphasis, for this essay, would be on "illegitimately." It seems an existential fact of minority life that one feels illegitimate, is made to feel illegitimate. Mexican writer Elena Poniatowska remarks that in a society hostile to women—and necessarily women writers—women are made to feel like freaks. "Isn't that a very refined, a very sophisticated form of repression?" Perhaps I was writing *Haunted Houses* "against" being a freak, at the same time I knew—and know—myself to be one, sitting there (here) writing.

Still, while I may want to un-man a language that reflects and produces conditions hostile to women, I don't imagine that I write a feminine language. I might have believed it possible, had I been a Frenchwoman who had learned to speak with *la* and *le* before masculine and feminine nouns, had this been part of my mother—my—tongue. But I wasn't. I haven't found another language to use; the language I was born into—and my inevitable blindnesses—is a limit I acknowledge. I've entered into one language (which from one point of view un-manned me) that has to be twisted around in order for me to make it work differently. As I write this I remember the Rorschach test I was given by a psychologist friend years ago. I didn't want her to find out anything about me, so I went through the cards quickly, insouciantly. When we were done, she said: "You didn't take this seriously, but one thing I can tell you—whichever way I gave you the cards, you took them and you read them. You never once turned the cards around or upside down. The way I handed them to you, that's the way you looked at them." It hadn't occurred to me to do it differently. Now it does. But perhaps this is the limit I accept—I'm handed this grammar, this alphabet, this language embedded with cultural nuances, and I try to turn it upside down, to shuffle it, a deck of cards to build houses of cards—stories, essays, novels.

As part of a reshuffling, I reread a white Western male writer, D.H. Lawrence, and found that his literary "discoverer," Ford Madox Ford, marked Lawrence's entrance into "literature" with a certain *parti pris*. Of Lawrence's story, "Odour of Chrysanthemums," Ford wrote: "You are, then, for as long as the story lasts, to be in one of those untidy, unfinished landscapes where locomotives wander innocuously amongst women with baskets . . . You are going to learn how what we used to call 'the other half'—though we might as well have said other ninety-nine hundredths—lives . . . Because this man knows . . . He knows the life he is writing about . . ." Ford, himself a white Western man, positions Lawrence in "the other half," where women, as one minority among many, might place themselves or be placed. But to Ford, from the upper classes, the working class was other, as was ninety-nine hundredths of humanity, "other" to his "we." I suppose it's that use of "we" that produces "others" like me, makes "us" illegitimate—a "we" Lawrence was subject to as well.

This excursion to Lawrence is meant to take another step, a

critical step, backward and forward, I hope, for I am just as anxious about totalizing "man" (and "American," and "white") as I am eager to decenter and defamiliarize him (them), by turning his (their) centrality into a question. If I totalize "man," I allow "women" to be totalized and essentialized—or American, black, white, gay, straight, Gambian, Indian, Japanese, and so on.

From this point of view, and others, too, it was extremely useful (and moving) to read Edward Said's essay on the Gulf War, written in the midst of it, in which he stated: "The time has come where we cannot simply accuse the West of Orientalism and racism—I realize I am particularly vulnerable on this point . . . There are many Wests, some antagonistic, some not, with which to do business . . . The converse is equally true, that there are many Arabs for Westerners and others to talk to." Reading his seminal work *Orientalism* some years ago, learning how "the Orient" had been invented, in a sense, by the West, I also recognized the problem he's referring to—the point of his "vulnerability"—presenting the West as monolithic. This recognition forced me to examine, and made me uncomfortably aware of, another of my vulnerabilities— how I, in the name of my version of feminism, had relied too heavily on "patriarchy," for one thing, for too many explanations.

So it's probably not surprising, given my concern with essentialisms of all kinds (and the construction of identity generally), that questioning national identity—how the nation state is inscribed in our different psyches, how each of us may be a repository of a national history and culture, how identity is inflected by nationality—that this was the impetus, even the mission (maybe impossible), for *Motion Sickness*, a novel whose narrator is a young, disquieted American woman traveling in Europe. But I have to admit, trying to be honest—although I question my ability to be honest—that I was also writing conscious of writing itself as a project, and that the desire to write *Motion Sickness*—the pleasure I derived from it, being its first reader—came from writing, and that the writing was of the utmost importance to me. I would never want to let go of that importance; it must coexist with the importance—to me—of what I think the book, the story, is about.

One writes in the cracks rather than by stepping over them, like a child playing a game as she walks on the sidewalk. My version: if I stepped on the crack, the line, I would die. Sometimes the rules of the game changed—I changed them, but rather paranoically: if I didn't step on the crack, I would die. Whatever the rule, the consequences were dire. Perhaps I didn't know how to play. I don't think I did. Maybe a portent, that child's game, of things to come. For while I can say I play with language, the game is dire, urgent, necessary. And the rules must change.

It's funny. Though skeptical and prone to depression, I write in the hope and spirit that each of us can think beyond our limits, while acknowledging limits. I picture us all, like Bakhtin's idea of the novel, with many possible voices, as dialogical as words. There are identities, there are shifting subjectivities, and you and I are shifty subjects who may from time to time be many things, not essentially any one thing, except by desire perhaps and in certain moments, for certain reasons and for certain periods of time. I really am looking for new narratives to replace the old ones. I distrust words and stories and yet probably they are what I value most. Paradox rules.

1991

3. Love Story

Derek Jarman's *Caravaggio* is not a *Masterpiece Theater* version of the life of a great painter. Its sets are minimal and sometimes anachronistic, as are some of the props and the dialogue, alluding as much to Italian Neorealist cinema as to the Counter-Reformation. In its approach to art history, in which the painter Caravaggio (1571–1610) is sometimes referred to as the last great Rennaissance master, Jarman's *Caravaggio* is insouciant, but not shocking if one believes that history is a matter of interpretation, of fighting over meaning, of imposing meaning. As Jarman himself puts it, in an interview in an English film magazine, "The past does not exist. It is what we interpret . . . When Caravaggio painted biblical scenes they were always of people in his period . . . It's only a recent tradition that creeps in by way of someone like Poussin who does it properly and makes it look like Rome . . . It seems to me very old-fashioned and unthinking the more recent way of visualizing films (about the past)".

As if to insist upon this dead or nonexistent past, the film opens with a shot of the dying Caravaggio. His face is scarred; one eye open, the other shut. He's gone, it appears, and this dying body frames the film and is its present tense, after which all other scenes are of the past—flashbacks. Or Caravaggesque scenes, tableaux, parading before the spectator's eyes as if they were Caravaggio's own death-rattle phantasms, the feverish visions of a dying artist.

Jarman uses certain agreed-upon facts of Caravaggio's short and controversial life and career for the film's narrative. Cardinal Del Monte, Caravaggio's patron, appears first in the film where he appears in art-history texts about the painter's life—beside the hospital bed of the young Caravaggio. Jarman also represents the artist Baglione, who wrote about Caravaggio in his *Lives*, published in 1642, and Scipione Borghese, a nephew of the Pope, who was a patron of the arts as well as a cardinal. How these, and other, historical figures are represented is another matter. Baglione types insults on a manual typewriter or sits like Marat in a bathtub, penning attacks. (In his book *Caravaggio*, Howard Hibbard writes that since Baglione "was himself a painter in Rome during this entire period, we have to take all his statements seriously." Jarman's approach—he is also a painter—seems the reverse: can we trust anything Baglione has to say about a fellow painter/competitor?) Scipione Borghese looks like a Mafia capo; the Pope whispers to Caravaggio about the painter's naughtiness as if the two were in sacrilegious cahoots. With these representations Jarman challenges received ideas about the past, which is itself already a series of representations.

In the broadest possible sense, *Caravaggio* translates a life into film. Thus all the elements that go toward making it a film called *Caravaggio*—its cinematography, its lighting, its dialogue, its art direction, its editing—represent Jarman's conception of Caravaggio. The aspect of Jarman's art that most intrigues me is the fiction he employs to tell Caravaggio's story. Jarman invents a character called Jerusaleme to be the painter's helper/son and builds a complicated fictitious relationship among three people, based upon two documented events: Caravaggio's murder of Ranuccio Thomasoni, and a court case involving Caravaggio in a fight over a woman called Lena, who was most likely a prostitute.

After the scene in which Caravaggio is shown dying, with his helper Jerusaleme in attendance, the first flashback is to Caravaggio paying money to a poor family for a six-year-old boy (who turns out to be Jerusaleme). The next scene is of the boy and the painter in his studio; the boy plays with Caravaggio's *Medusa*, using it as a shield as he runs around the room. Next the boy climbs into the lap of Caravaggio, who strokes his hair tenderly and rocks him in his arms. Jerusaleme is mute, dumb. Like a fool that Shakespeare— whose dates are roughly equivalent to Caravaggio's—might have created, he watches devotedly over his master's life as he grows up with him. Through his silence he acts as Caravaggio's silent partner, standing in for the ineffable, the unspoken. At times he literally appears to be Caravaggio's other half. Another interpretation: his presence in Caravaggio's life challenges the conventional view of the painter as a violent man, and perhaps challenges a view of homosexuals that would not allow them to be good paternal or maternal figures. Or perhaps his silence represents the impossibility of bringing back history. The mute is an unsettling presence in the film, as much an audience to the events as the maker who tries to film dead events and people.

Jarman's film attempts to match and parallel his sense of the painter's style. His choice of actors to play Caravaggio's models is idiosyncratic, as was Caravaggio's—he used poor people, street toughs, prostitutes to pose for religious subjects. For lighting Jarman incorporates Caravaggio's innovative chiaroscuro, making a rich color film that's reminiscent of black-and-white Hollywood films of the '40s, with their emphasis on shadow, white whites, and black blacks. But unlike classic cinema, where there is either a good girl or a femme fatale or sometimes both, in *Caravaggio* sexual jealousy and pleasure are spread generously in a different kind of sexual economy among the three protagonists of the fictitious love affair that Jarman gives us.

Jarman could have fashioned an ordinary triangular relationship, where one of the lovers does not get a share of the love in circulation. Instead, he has constructed a relationship of complicated feelings, actions, and looks that turns into a treatise on sexuality and sexual politics in the artist's time, and our own. In classic cinema, according to Laura Mulvey in her oft-quoted "Visual Pleasure and Narrative Cinema", one of the three looks of the cinema is the look of the male protagonist at the female protagonist, which fixes her as the object of the gaze. In *Caravaggio*, in almost every scene in which the three lovers—Ranuccio is a street fighter with whom Caravaggio falls in love and who models for him; Lena is initially Ranuccio's lover—appear together, each character looks from one to the other. The male characters are as much fixed by Lena's gaze as they are by each other's and she is by theirs. When Caravaggio kisses Ranuccio on the mouth, Lena is present and watching. When Caravaggio presents Lena with a beautiful ball gown to wear to an art opening (called an unveiling), Lena's kiss of delight for Caravaggio turns into one of passion, as Ranuccio watches in the background, somewhat out of focus but in the frame. After they break from their embrace, both turn to look at him, which is followed by a shot of his looking at them. In fact when Caravaggio first approaches Ranuccio, Lena is there, and what could have been a close-up of Ranuccio alone as looked at by Caravaggio is a medium shot of Ranuccio and Lena as looked at by him. This structure of complicated looks is repeated over and over again.

Ultimately Lena leaves Ranuccio for Scipione Borghese, telling Ranuccio in front of Caravaggio, "You have Michele." She is pregnant, and when Ranuccio asks whose child it is, she answers, "Mine." She smiles and proclaims that her child will be very, very rich. Ranuccio appears stunned; Caravaggio watchful, reflective. The next scene is of Lena's drowned body floating in a river. (From the script: "Like Ophelia, she is dressed in a scarlet gown which streams out from her, turning, turning, an image of peace and beauty at rest.") From the moment of her death, the film spirals from death to death. Ranuccio tells Caravaggio that he killed Lena for him, "for love," and Caravaggio slits his lover's throat. Soon after Caravaggio finally dies.

Jarman's *Caravaggio* imagines a time that Foucault theorizes about in *The History of Sexuality*, a time when sexuality was less scrutinized and less controlled. Caravaggio, like Shakespeare, partook of the spirit of his age, an age that allowed for sexual ambiguity, in which sexuality and identity were not so closely aligned that one could not sometimes be with men or with women. Shakespeare's sonnets and comedies, in particular, attest to this. And while sodomy, according to Foucault, has always been treated as an aberration, it was the act rather than the person that was aberrant.

The killing of Ranuccio by Caravaggio is a stunning and disturbing act. It says, for one thing, that Caravaggio will not love over this woman's dead body. It's a scene that Thomas Hoving, in his review of the film for *Connoisseur* (1986) titled "A Question of Vulgarity," finds more violent than all the killing in Sylvester Stallone's *Cobra*, which Hoving contrasts to Jarman's film. *Cobra*, Hoving writes, "isn't vulgar or cynical. It's a straightforward, taut, well-crafted celluloid romp. The slaughter is so clean and unaffecting that you cannot take it seriously . . . I wish I could say as much for *Caravaggio*." Hoving continues: "No one knows whether Caravaggio was homosexual. Nevertheless, the director has seized upon this speculation as if it were the absolute truth, and the film *slithers on* from there" (italics added). I mention this review, not for its insights, but for its patent homophobia. Jarman has called *Caravaggio* "a public statement", and it seems to me its statement is in part directed toward comments such as Hoving's.

I've chosen to concentrate primarily on *Caravaggio* the love story rather than on *Caravaggio* the artist story, which is also a significant part of this elegant and intelligent film. Jarman cuts from scenes of the painter's life to the scenes he painted from life. Some of the most arresting images in the film are the groupings of models, absolutely still, holding their poses, which by now are famous through Caravaggio's paintings of them. Jarman did not film the paintings themselves; instead, they are represented in the film by posed tableaux, and by Christopher Hobb's paintings of the paintings. Caravaggio's friends, lovers and patrons have been incorporated into these tableaux: Cardinal Del Monte poses for *St. Jerome in His Study*, and Ranuccio Thomasoni for *The*

Martyrdom of St. Matthew. By showing Caravaggio at work on these tableaux, Jarman constantly animates the paintings by moving into the artist's life to demonstrate where his work came from. When the streetwise models for *Concert of Youths* break their pose, they kid Caravaggio about his relations with Cardinal Del Monte. For Jarman's Caravaggio, the life that informed his art is more valuable than the art itself; midway through the film Jarman has Caravaggio say, "How can you compare flesh and blood with oil and ground pigment?"

What I've written about, however, is what *Caravaggio* "meant" to me. And I add my interpretation to other possible interpretations, all of which are based upon Jarman's representations of other interpretations, and participate in a seemingly endless love affair and battle with meaning.

1987

4.

Like Rockets and Television

In choosing the pictures for this book, I asked myself: If you didn't know who any of these people were, would that still be an interesting picture?

—Stephen Shore

This book is possible, not because the people are interesting, but because the photographs are.

—Sterling Morrison

Andy was difficult. I mean, it was great to be with him. He was cheap and impossible some days. I consider him a genius, I guess. Whatever that means.

—Taylor Mead

I feel I'm very much part of my times, of my culture, as much a part of it as rockets and television.

—Andy Warhol[1]

1. Gretchen Berg, "Nothing to Lose: Interview with Andy Warhol." *Cahiers du Cinema* (*English*), (May 1967): 40. The other quotes are from interviews with the author.

Many people were drawn to Andy Warhol and the Factory. For some, he and it were the New York scene of the sixties. The cast of characters in these photographs, who acted in his films, worked with him, hung around his second studio on East 47th Street, was diverse. Gerald Malanga, Billy Name, Ondine, Brigid Berlin, Paul Morrissey. The Velvet Underground—discovered and showcased by Warhol as part of the "Exploding Plastic Inevitable" at the Dom on St. Marks Place: John Cale, Sterling Morrison, Lou Reed, Maureen Tucker, and singer Nico, a legend in their own time. The other Factory band, not a rock group, originated from Cambridge/Harvard: Edie Sedgwick, Donald Lyons, Danny Fields, Gordon Baldwin, Dorothy Dean, Edmund Hennessy, Ed Hood, Chuck Wein. (It's possible, not probable, that years from now three twentieth-century Cambridges will be cited—Wittgenstein's, Blunt's, the Factory's.) There were Mary (Might) Woronov, Ultra Violet, Pat Hartley, Susan Bottomly/International Velvet, Henry Geldzahler, Jonas Mekas, Sam Green.

For varying amounts of time, with varying degrees of involvement, each had a part in Warhol's studio or world—before he was shot and nearly killed by Valerie Solanas on June 3, 1968. Things changed then. He changed, the Factory changed. They were never the same again.

This book of photographs and words, visual and verbal images, represents the Factory before that assassination attempt, an act familiar in the sixties, almost appropriate to the decade. In fact, Warhol was shot the day before Robert F. Kennedy was assassinated. A morbid syncopation, Warhol shared headlines with the murdered RFK, took the lower half of the newspaper, suitable to his somewhat scandalous, underground, artistic status.

Shore's photographs coincide in time with Warhol's emergence as a prominent artist. They also mark the middle to near-end of Warhol's active filmmaking career. In 1965 Warhol formally resigned from painting, to concentrate on filmmaking. In 1968 Warhol informally resigned from filmmaking and handed over the directional reins to Paul Morrissey. But not until he finished *Blue Movie*, a tremulous, exhausting because exhaustive, beautifully shot portrait of a sexual relationship—skin; bodies; tender, playful talk—a romantic and wry afternoon-into-evening celluloid affair. As intimate a view of sex and love as ever produced for the screen, a uniquely private look for public consumption, it uncannily corresponds with Warhol's withdrawal from filmmaking, into a less public Factory. The old Factory, as it came to be called, had been a "permissive" space—apropos the sixties—an open space, everyone says.

> Dean of Poppycock Art, he of the Brillo Boxes and Campbell's Soup Cans . . .
> his own oozing degeneracy . . .
> this Warhol type is vulgar, meaningless, obscene, and an unmitigated, outrageous bore . . .
> NY Court Finds Warhol's "Blue Movie" Obscene; Att'y Says He'll Appeal.[2]

Will quotes like these be relegated to eccentric responses, historical footnotes? Will it be remembered that once upon a time Warhol and his work were regarded as decadent, outrageous, obscene, silly? Will a disreputable Warhol be saved? (In the same *Variety* article cited above, Warhol is quoted as saying: "Kids today are so far beyond simple sex that it's only the middle-aged who are upset, because they can't reconcile sex with their own blighted lives.")

In the sixties Andy Warhol was a defiant, uncomfortable public presence. His art discomforted from early in its initial phases, defamiliarizing and reframing cultural objects and social facts: electric chairs, Marilyn, Jackie, car crashes, Elvis, Campbell's Soup cans, Liz Taylor, black people being attacked by police dogs in the South. In making a mark on different things American, Warhol chose promiscuity. This seeming lack of "taste" or "discrimination"

2. Eugene Boe, *Status*, March 1965, p. 71; *Chicago Daily News*, June 6, 1967; Harry MacArthur, *Washington Star*, April 29, 1967; *Variety* headline, September 24, 1969, respectively.

between so-called high and low culture, between serious and trivial, has been designated Camp, his scavenging of everyday objects and signs, Pop. But his ecumenicism, his range, that catholic appetite, was anything but a lack. His scavenging was emphatic, his "lacks" not absences but presences in his work, a thoroughgoing strategy, a point of view, a way of seeing and thinking.

If anyone showed how weird the idea of taste is, it was Warhol. His various desires, or tastes, often seemed in conflict with each other. He collected everything, had shopping bags full of unopened packages in his house at his death. He wanted things, just to have them, he liked to look, long and longingly.

He was a cultural omnivore, a culture vulture, who went forth and multiplied. He produced serial images instead of pristine objects whose value was in their one-of-a-kindness. Seriality changed art, the way one looked at art; simultaneously it interacted with changing social ideas, as the world turned, to title it soap opera.

While he ripped up the social carpet, his work proposed a different social/art contract. He broke hallowed aesthetic ground. He replaced one kind of image with another, with others. His replacement images may now even appear to be "natural," expected outcomes of our mediated lives, the way things are, or were meant to be, always around, second nature, second sight. His work is difficult, though, if one lets it be, just because it can easily be taken at face value. It questions what one is looking at merely by being on the wall, being looked at by you. Also the work is beautiful, ugly, ambiguous, perverse, uncanny. Uncanny, a pun on his soup cans maybe. Even if they no longer shock, they still may surprise. Though perhaps there's no way that a stack of Brillo boxes or a dollar sign, even on the wall of a gallery or museum, certainly a film of a still thing like the Empire State Building, will ever be art for some people—and that may contribute to their power as images.

Not completely assimilable in the world they were meant to intervene in, or fit into, not whole-some, not yet, they still hang in museums and now have a museum to themselves in Pittsburgh, where Warhol himself didn't want to hang. One day, maybe, he'll be like Renoir, a father of Popular Art. Already he and his work are pieces of the built environment—the wallpaper around us—which he helped design. Ironically it may be the reason why he's a little lost, he's so much in it, one can't see him and his influence, he's too much around.

Like Caravaggio's, his shocking, dirty past needs remembering, not enshrining, not sanitizing. In the sixties, Warhol was considered a freak, dangerous to the community. Some recognized early the importance of his work; most didn't. He was an artist provocateur, an early warning to the system of things to come. That was his appeal, in part, to the people who spent time with him in the Factory. His difference, his indifference, his queerness, his conformity, his contrariness, his charisma, his passivity, his activity. The word "conformity" is dated, except when talking about the Army. Did Warhol have a part in that, did his work signify that everyone was a little conformist, there was no escape from the system? Did he revel in conformity, his own version—success, beauty, money, social status—as he rebelled against it, parodied it? Isn't parody one part love, the other hate?

Warhol's own system relied on making a lot of a little. Making a *faux* Hollywood studio in a loft. Using a repeated repertoire of images and a repertory company that didn't act. Or didn't act right. Making a film of a man sleeping. A film of a young woman talking to an off-screen voice. Or showing a haircut in process, men staring at the camera. He was erotically invested in looking, ambivalent about being looked at. Serial imagery allows a longer look, makes a lot out of one image. Warhol thought the viewer wanted to be able, or forced, to look longer, too. He directed a 25-hour-long film **** (*Four Stars*), projected it on two screens with superimpositions, so it was actually 50 hours of film. He wanted to film *The Warhol Bible*; each page of the Bible would be projected on the screen long enough to be read by the audience. A 30-day movie.

His desire to do and have it all was grand, his need to encompass and compass big. Great. If he's a great artist, it has to do with this and with how many meanings and values—qualities—one can find or discard in his work. He, though, didn't want to discard anything,

he wanted to use everything. Waste not, want not, applies nicely
to him, a Catholic/Puritan.

No wastrel, he appropriated pictures from an image-heavy world.
Warhol mocked categories, high and low, and deified both; he
flattened, flattered, teased, ironed out or ironized both sides of an
argument. He did it in such a dialectical manner, one wonders
what makes something one or the other. Work/play, art/commerce,
gay/straight, candid/posed, male/female, sexual/asexual, moral/
amoral, masculine/feminine, scripted/unscripted, boring/exciting,
upper/lower, progressive/reactionary, political/apolitical, traditional/
modern, individual genius/historical moment, original/influenced,
art/politics, form/content—simple oppositions are disturbed in
Warhol's world. His work can be viewed through any, if not all, of
these frames and claims. Meaning, there's something to argue about.

It wasn't his queerness alone that set him apart, though his
queerness absolutely affected his practice. It wasn't his reading
comics in bed and listening to the radio when he was a sickly
child, lying there, cutting out pictures and daydreaming, it wasn't
just this that determined him. But it was a part of what set him on
his way. It wasn't only having been a commercial artist, but it was
part of how he went. It wasn't only that his mother adored him,
encouraged him, but it was a big part of it. It wasn't only that the
sixties was fraught, convulsive, but he was a part of that, and it a
part of him. Insecure and arrogant, a prolific worker, a heavy-duty
shopper, a hard worker who partied hard, or so it's said by some,
disclaimed by others—what's left of Andy Warhol is his work.
Paintings, prints, photographs, films, books. Famous, he's different,
but like everybody else, it's hard to know who he really was. Still,
it would be a strange myopia not to recognize his shape in and on
things, his effect.

Subversive, transgressive, these words are tossed like salads,
hyperbolic and sexy window dressing. Warhol was a mixer, he
mixed it up and contributed to the cultural brew and cultural
critique. A social artist, a social climber, a working-class boy, his
Factory (no worker's paradise but better than most factories), his
paintings and films paraded differences, even class differences in a

country that prides itself on being classless. In films such as *Bike Boy*, Warhol irreverently exposed the contradiction in a big way.

Irreverence, of course, depends on reverence. Warhol's insistence on using one roll of film for a scene or his use of the same image again and again shows a reverence for his material, that roll of film, that particular pose. Or reverence for the formal ideas he adhered to and employed. Within the different contexts he worked, he played with his medium. He shot "sexploitation" movies for porn houses that were not about cum shots, not particularly "sexploitative". He filled an art gallery with silver helium pillows, making art ephemera, or ephemeral, inflated, a joke, a game, or a hoax. Or just as likely an idea about space. Openly homosexual, even flamboyant when the closet was shut, Warhol was one of the first, if not the first—excluding television's Uncle Miltie Berle—to bring transvestites, drag queens, into mainstream culture in the US.

Two actions especially represent an anarchic, defiant Warhol. In 1956, Warhol tried to join the Tanager Gallery, an artists' cooperative that included Philip Pearlstein, the painter, an old friend from Pittsburgh, where Warhol was born. Warhol submitted a painting of a group of boys kissing. He—it—was rejected.

"The other members of the gallery hated and refused to show [it]," Pearlstein said. "He felt hurt and he didn't understand. I told him I thought the subject matter was treated too aggressively, too importantly" and that was "probably the last time we were in touch".[3]

Did Warhol expect acceptance? Was he naive? Was his disappointment at being rejected or in discovering that artists were, like everyone else, limited? Was his action an unconscious statement, an aesthetic one? None of the above? Calculatedly or unconsciously he followed his desire, put it in his work, strutted his stuff, showed agency.

3. Philip Pearlstein, quoted in David Bourdon, *Warhol*. Harry N. Abrams, Inc., 1989. p.51.

In 1964 Philip Johnson, the architect, asked Warhol to decorate the New York State Pavilion for the World's Fair building, which Johnson had designed. Warhol produced *Thirteen Most Wanted Men*, meant to grace the outside of the building—thirteen criminals in profile and full face. Decoration for a state building. The image was rejected, as might have been expected and intended; then Warhol proposed a replacement—cover the building with images of Robert Moses, the World's Fair director. This sweetly perverse reversal of positions was also rejected. In the end Warhol painted over *Thirteen Most Wanted Men* in his signature aluminium/silver paint. The wanted men obscured, made obscene, they were set against the state, or under it, as a palimpsest. They were the literal underworld of the state, a physical layer residing in the state.

It's an uncanny rebellion. Max Weber defined the state as that institution alone legitimated to kill. Some of the Most Wanted Men must have committed murder, a practice reserved for the state. So the preserve of art and the preserve of the state met on the surface of the building and had a silvered fate, were a turn of events, like that which the flip of a coin might produce, as flip as a coin flip, those changed positions or fates. *Most Wanted Men*'s other provocation is sexual, challenging the state with an outlaw, unspeakable love, homosexuality, to haunt it as underbelly. Warhol, queer-American, gives new meaning to the phrase "self-made man." A self made into any man, bad, good, as random an end as the flip of that coin.

Ordinary things could have value, quality; conversely, paintings by Old Masters or characters who came over on the Mayflower could be merely superficial, with surface values and no more meaning—quality—than a picture of a banana. If so, artists themselves might not be valuable, because the product questions its producer. With this kind of destruction, or reconsideration, with his bad attitude, Warhol danced the Twist with the sanctity of art and artist. He may never entirely be forgiven, as if he were one of the Manson family, another sixties phenomenon.

He courted fame, visibility. On the face of it, he was shameless. On the face of it, he was tantalized by famous faces, brazenly invested in notoriety. He lusted for things, appeared awkward, thought he was ugly, encouraged others in exposing their peculiarities and troubles, especially in his movies. Criminals, or Jackies, Marilyns, or *Poor Little Rich Girls* like Edie Sedgwick, *Bike Boys* like Joe Spencer were sources—of inspiration, of pleasure—for him. Lou Reed might say Warhol walked on the wild side. But his embodiment of artist was also strategic, effective. An art star/art businessman, Warhol's image was not that of a wild and crazy libertine, a bohemian, or an isolated, tortured painter. He bedevilled the picture of the artist as much as he did art. Maybe this will stand as the most outrageous of his services/disservices— his threat to that order of things.

There are those who aren't interested in Warhol's work, don't get the picture, never did or will, find or see nothing, no qualities, in it, none at all in him. This reminds me of Leonard Woolf's defense of Virginia Woolf's writing. He didn't mind when people didn't like her books; he minded when they said they weren't about anything. An argument over "quality" names the debate over meaning and values, social and aesthetic value. Assert something's value, its supposedly high quality, and one is insisting that an object has achieved the condition of meaningfulness.

Warhol was a canny artist, extreme, not a con artist. (His work may not promote confidence in anything, but that's a different matter.) He knew what he was doing, was self-conscious, no doubt counterphobic. He had a nose job, wore a wig, went out in open disguise, never really disguised his wants. Sexual desire flares in his art and his films. He queered things in lots of ways. There's no universal American, though Warhol was, as much as anyone could be, an American artist. By now, he's even an American artifact. Emphasize queer, he's a hyphenated American. Hyphens upset universality, the idea we're all the same, or that art is a universal medium everyone everywhere can understand. Hyphens punctuate the universe with specificity, and in the specific, in the detail, is another detail. Flaubert wrote, "Life is in the details."

Esquire asked me in a questionnaire who would I like to

have play me, and I answered Edie Sedgwick, because she does everything better than I do. It was just a surface question, so I gave them a surface answer.

—Andy Warhol[4]

I use the frame as a way of deciding what I want to include in the picture.

—Stephen Shore

To repeat, to make more of it, many people were drawn to Warhol and the Factory. These photographs confirm that, obviously. People are framed in all kinds of scenes—on film shoots, in individual portraits, candid shots, formal ones, in groups, working, kidding around. The frame is an embrace, a lover's decision, and like any embrace, something's included, something's excluded. The frame necessarily excludes more than it includes. There's another world, worlds, outside the perimeter of a photograph; what one sees is the result of focus, a point of view.

The Factory itself was a frame, including, excluding. It was a part of the sixties "counter-culture," but counter to much of that too. Maybe Warhol's Factory was countercounterculture, not as straight, more on the couch than on the bus or road. There's a cast of characters and a stage, the Factory, on which they perform, pose, or act themselves in front of Shore's camera. The period—its conflicts, customs—surfaces sometimes obliquely in these photographs. What's not seen, not in the Factory, not in the picture, also reverberates. The viewer may intrude into the picture plane, place oneself in or out, fill in the blanks. One interprets, projects, fantasizes, imagines, identifies, remembers or doesn't.

Thinking about it, I wondered: is the Factory, now that it's gone, just a place, a physical space, or a historical space, a mental space, a frame of mind? History works at a remove, carrying the past into the present, so it's different from the way it was to the people

4. Berg, "Nothing to Lose," p.40.

living in it. By figuring the Factory and Warhol in pictures and words—a litany of representations—they are both transformed, take new forms. But they can't be other than history. Or images and words. As these photographs imply, full of immediacy and fully at a remove, there's no way back to life in the Factory.

So I decided to interview some of the people who appear in Shore's photographs, to ask them about the Factory, Warhol, themselves, issues in Warhol's work, how they saw things. Supposedly Warhol said that Edison and silent movies influenced his filmmaking most. I wanted to preserve the silence of a photograph, how it doesn't speak in words, and also to include with these silent, vivid images human voices. I came to think of the people I interviewed—some I knew, some I got to know—as the Speakers. That turned the project into a novel of resonant pictures, resilient voices. I dropped myself out of the interviews, fashioned them into prose narratives, and let the edited texts stand as stories, not answers. The stories, other kinds of images, don't translate the pictures into words. The photographs don't illustrate the stories.

I sometimes hoped that the Factory characters of thirty years ago would burst out of this pictured past, break that silence, say their piece, at least part of it, even shatter their images. I found myself asking one of the speakers: Do you remember what you were feeling or thinking then, at that moment? He didn't, of course. I was caught, longing—to return to the moment, the scene, the time. It's something one can't do; but one of the uncanny effects of an arresting photograph is to offer as here and now something distant and gone. Photographs catch one wanting, trying to interpret, to understand and read into. None can be taken at face value, as if telling unambiguous tales. Photographs may be palpable reminders of what's not remembered, not said. They are imprints, prints truly, documents as much of absence as presence. And even more weirdly, photographs sometimes seem to supply what's missing, by offering something to look at that's not there, another composition, a fiction. I couldn't stop looking at these pictures, which make room for history, doubt, beauty, curiosity, uneasiness, satisfaction, solemnity.

They're analogues to life in the Factory, existing in a specular and speculative relationship to it. The portraits and pairings, the group shots, the images of a young Warhol, provide spaces for reflection about a recent past, about images themselves, about an image itself. The pose, after all, was an important element in Warhol's world.

Death is the frame with the toughest grip, with an embrace for everyone. Warhol's death—and others in the photographs—frames him. Now a dead artist/celebrity, maybe he's even more famous. Alive, he'd be a different picture. There'd be some potential for his changing his image. At the least, one looks at pictures of the dead differently. People talk about the dead differently. There's that saying, don't speak ill of the dead. I wondered how Andy Warhol would've been spoken about by the speakers if he were alive. People might have talked differently. Maybe not. For most, enough time had passed for dispassionate reflection. But death can alter memory, shake it up, harden or soften it or both. Memory is selective, inventive, human—it shares all our other characteristics. Death has a habit of reinventing the past and present. In Shore's photographs and in the speakers' words, Warhol's present, absent, alive as living memory. Sometimes memory wrestles with history. Sometimes both are defeated. Sometimes it's hard to know what really happened. Or what it meant that it happened, in the past.

One of the mandates of the avant-garde, which Warhol broke from, was to be ahead of one's time and to know in what way one was. Shifting into the postmodern, one is pressed to learn how to think, live, work, breathe the present—even if it's inescapable, like inhaling an unrecuperable past. It's harder to live in and think the present than be ahead of it; there's no exit. It's no aesthetic failing to be in time, with it. The imaginary future is always there and not there, to envision or make up, to wonder and worry about, to live into and even for.

When Roland Barthes wrote "The Death of the Author," he didn't kill any authors. You'd think he had. Some have anyway been narcissistically wounded. Authors/artists are implicated, entangled, in a world of images, written and oral languages. Barthes didn't kill agency, uniqueness, genius; although recognizing that one's sometimes brilliant or dumb, boring or exciting thought and life is a group activity can be murder. The irony is that as Warhol helped undo and unsettle ideas about originality, he himself was inventive, unique, "an original." It's no paradox. The frame, or context, fixes and unfixes interpretation. A photograph, painting, movie, or novel, jettisoned into a future where nothing can be known for sure, lands shakily on different ground. Meaning is wild, uncontrollable. Just as any artist's legacy is. Just as Warhol's is. No one is ordinary or everybody is, profoundly. That's a kind of ambivalent tribute to Warhol, and maybe it's attributable to him.

1995

5.

My Funny
Ambivalence

I walked by a bar on St. Marks Place on March 21, right after St. Patrick's Day, and a large sign was still up: Forget about progress/ Enjoy a Traditional St. Patrick's Day Party Here. It led me from one twisty narrative to another.

The sign "Enjoy a Traditional St. Patrick's Day" dares to comfort those who don't care or don't want to care whether homosexuals are allowed to march in the St. Patrick's Day Parade. Progress is a dirty word here; it ruins fun, traditional fun. Is fun always traditional? One doesn't have to believe in progress to understand the problem the sign disposes of: thinking about one's homophobia, thinking about the other, or thinking about one's limits. To have to think like that is to be forced out of one's enjoyment or comfort.

Then I thought about jokes, which are little stories, and shock jocks and comics, and jokes that are offensive to me, or jokes that are mean and funny, jokes that are not offensive, jokes that are just bad or stupid. Is this humor, are these guys comforting, because it and they celebrate, not recognize, limits or being limited? Do the guys wallow, revel and have a party in their limits? Console some of us in our confusion about and in the midst of change? Let some of us breathe easier about "freely" expressing those supposedly bad things, the bad parts of us? The so-called unacknowledged truth inside us?

I began wondering about the popularity of *Schindler's List*. Because around all these thoughts is the question: Who is allowed to be a victim? Who may call themselves oppressed? There's a specter hovering over this land—it's a common, deep ambivalence toward victims. One hates what one may become against one's will, one hates the degraded, the disgusting, one feels powerless and hates anyone who evidences that powerlessness. One would rather identify with the aggressor, to use Anna Freud's formulation.

Then I thought that *Schindler's List*'s popularity has little or nothing to do with the Holocaust, but everything to do with the context, the times, in which it is being viewed or received. *Schindler's List* has nothing to do with antisemitism, racism; there is never any discussion of why this terror is happening to the Schindler Jews, with the exception of the sadomasochism of one German concentration camp "director," an explanation that is both reductive and misuses psychoanalysis. One needs a psychoanalytic interpretation along with, not in place of, an ideological one, which is what I'm trying to assert here.

Returning to the question of the victim in this twisty narrative: I'll suggest that many Americans—troubled, fearful, depressed, unsure—may be able to identify with nameless Jews, who are presented as real, legitimate victims. And even more, many Americans may want to be legitimated as victims, as oppressed, as hostages to an uncertain fate, as subjects in need of a savior—America's place in the world, culturally, economically, politically, is drastically different from what it was after that war. Oskar Schindler is the knight on the white horse—he does even sit on a horse and look down from a hillside as Jews are being rounded up and murdered; and Schindler does indeed save some of them—a relative few. Narratively speaking, Schindler is ET, or the good sheriff who saves the townsfolk from the evil gang.

What about the popularity of the Holocaust Museum? If one

takes drug choice as an indicator, isn't it telling that in the heady, postwar fifties middle-class Americans took speed, not to get high; now it's Prozac. Read this way, people in this country are desperate, depressed, at a loss; it's more than economic. Where better to go than to a movie that offers a savior. Or to a museum where there is, to use Primo Levi's term, no gray zone. The journey to the museum or the museum journey, which was conceived as telling the story of the Holocaust, may articulate what one may be feeling, but what one cannot say about one's life—it is a failure. Everything I hoped for is lost. I need a place to mourn. As the Holocaust Museum's designer said in a TV documentary, "We tried to tell the story from the victim's perspective."

I turn on the TV, and every talk show is debating the credibility and plight of a variety of victims. Simultaneously, there's a celebration, trivialization, and exploitation of the speakers. Again to paraphrase Primo Levi: these people are not allowed to bear witness. Instead they must often defend their right to be recognized as victims; TV is the court of last resort. It's the current fascination and disease—spot the victim, decide if it is allowed to be named victim, despise the victim, pin the tail on the victim, identify with the victim, revile the victim, have sympathy or disgust for the victim. Our responses are ambivalent, filled with frustrated identifications and projections.

Which led me to wonder again about *Schindler's List* in our present context: Who will be allowed to be "the Jew of the Holocaust" in our current narrative? That is, who will be allowed to occupy that position—that space—to be permitted to say, "I have a legitimate grievance in this land. It's not debatable." I am not and would never deny the uniqueness of the Holocaust. What I'm raising by this question has to do with thinking about and understanding the twistiness of stories with which one identifies, with a desire toward avoiding the prioritization of suffering, toward moving more generously, whoever we are, even with our ambivalence intact. But to share suffering is one of the hardest things to do.

Which is why the question of who is allowed to be a victim—

whether in terms of rape or racism or other discrimination and abuse—is with us. And the question asks how to think about victimage, whether even to think about it, whether to allow others to mess up our fun, whether to think about fun like that, how and when to take pleasure.

Other people hurt, or you do. You realize that you may contribute to others pain, at the same time that you too are hurting. One may defend oneself against any of these thoughts. One may be a victim, sometimes, and sometimes, in some instances, a victimizer, a perp. Our ideology argues that anyone can make it here. Blame the victim starts there.

I don't want to blame victims—I'm purposely using a hackneyed phrase—even if I occasionally laugh at mean, crude, or indifferent jokes. Jokes permit a safer sadism. There is a difference between laughing at a joke—jokes are as complex and puzzling as dreams, Freud teaches—and acting as if that response is the only reality, the only truth, and acting as if there is nothing to worry about, because one can and does laugh. Perhaps what I'm saying is that one must permit oneself one's fantasies, one's mental nastinesses, one's contradictory responses, but one will not, hopefully, imagine that that's the truth, the whole story. There is no whole story, and there is no one story for all of us, which is why some jokes are funny to some and not to others.

Anyone can be the victim of a joke, which in a way makes a comic democracy or democracy comic. Offense is the other side of defense. Laughter is as true and as false as tears, and sometimes similar. One's fantasies, dreams, jokes, and spontaneous emissions may be unvarnished and true in their ways. But other material that is also true or meaningful may take a great deal of work and thought to realize or articulate; this material may not necessarily spring unbridled out of us. Why is one kind of work or response privileged over another? I rely on the concept of the unconscious. But the unconscious is not an excuse; it is what is repressed. What one expresses deliberately is equally important. It is what one is ultimately responsible for. And to make matters even more complicated, each of us may have a different version of responsibility. Still, the unconscious mustn't be privileged over the conscious for facile purpose. Both speak truths, partial truths, and neither gives the whole story. That always eludes us.

1994

6. The Pleasure Principle

Jane Austen wrote, "One half of the world cannot understand the pleasures of the other." When I ask the director Chantal Akerman why she was attracted to the musical genre (which she used in her films *Les années 80/The Eighties* and *Window Shopping*), she answers, "Because it's so weird to express yourself without any rules. There is a convention, but you can say more about reality in an unrealistic way. I always like that. It gives me pleasure. It's about pleasure and freedom."

Pleasure and its vicissitudes, freedom and its constraints are key concepts in Akerman's work, consisting of 22 films in 21 years. Born in Brussels, in 1950, she decided to become a filmmaker when she was 15, after seeing Jean-Luc Godard's *Pierrot le fou*. She directed her first film, *Saute ma ville*, a short, in 1968, and by the time she was 24 had made the uncompromising *Je . . . Tu . . . Il . . . Elle* (1974).

For Akerman, the road to pleasure is paved, if not with pain, with frustration. *Je . . . Tu . . . Il . . . Elle* opens with the protagonist (Akerman herself) lying naked on a bed, eating frantically from a bag of sugar, and then writing a letter. There is no voice-over, no dialogue, just the presence of this inordinately hungry and voluptuous young woman. Finally, she leaves the room and goes on the road, hitching a ride with a truckdriver. He takes her on his journey, during which she masturbates him, off-camera. At the end of the day, she arrives at the apartment of another woman, perhaps the one she was writing the letter to. They eat, argue, then make love. The love scene is compelling not just because it explicitly shows a sexual encounter, but also because of Akerman's decision to keep the camera at a distance, from which it steadily records the lovers. The scene lasts so long that the pleasure of looking turns into unsatisfying and self-conscious voyeurism. From the first image of gluttony in *Je . . . Tu . . . Il . . . Elle*, Akerman brings us full circle by presenting a menu of appetites for sex, food, and life itself.

In the seventies, Akerman concentrated on the themes of motherhood, sexuality, domesticity, adventure, and female autonomy in what may be regarded as a trilogy: *Jeanne Dielman, News from Home,* and *Les Rendez-vous d'Anna*. Delphine Seyrig stars as a middle-class housewife, mother, and prostitute in the 225-minute *Jeanne Dielman*. The film portrays three days in Jeanne's life, dwelling on the monotony of a woman's household routine. Jeanne switches lights on and off, makes beds and meals, kisses her son, and opens the door to a man who turns out to be her trick of the day. Without missing a beat, she moves from one role to another, always in control of herself and her domain. The camera frames Jeanne with a fixity that matches her containment in all of her roles. The faint smile of this Mona Lisa, a bourgeoise manquée, fades after Jeanne has an orgasm with her second client. This unexpected, uncontrolled pleasure disturbs her; she comes out of the bedroom and her hair is mussed. She fumbles with the button of her robe. Her routine is now completely upset, and by the third day, she is unable to perform her tasks. At the end of the film, she murders her third client with sewing scissors, an act committed as dispassionately as if she were washing the dishes. The last shot is of Jeanne sitting at the dining-room table staring vacantly into space.

Delphine Seyrig's control and enigmatic beauty serve Akerman's minimalism perfectly. "Chantal is of her time," says Seyrig emphatically. "While other filmmakers do 19th-century filmmaking most of the time, hers is 20th-century filmmaking. That's why I think she's important. She, Ulrike Ottinger, and Marguerite Duras are really the people who are making movies modern."

Through Akerman's meticulous lens in *News from Home*, the adventure of leaving home and traveling to a foreign place—in this case, New York—becomes a meditation on how place is determined by absence as well as presence. The camera surveys the streets of Manhattan or stands resolutely in a subway station while Akerman reads her mother's letters on the soundtrack. Juxtaposed to the cityscape, the words counter the image through a maternal voice that disrupts what is seen on the screen.

In *Les Rendez-vous d'Anna*, the last film of this informal trilogy, Aurore Clement plays Anna, an "independent" filmmaker, touring Europe with her latest movie. She listens to the people she meets, some strangers, some friends, as they describe life in postwar Europe, especially the plight of its remaining Jews. Anna's relative silence functions like that of a psychoanalyst who hears the traumas of others and intervenes every so often just to let the analysand know she is there. The exquisite centerpiece of *Les Rendez-vous d'Anna* comes when the filmmaker meets her mother (Lea Massari) in a restaurant. They take a hotel room and lie close to each other on the bed, Anna revealing herself to her mother the way the people she had met on her tour had done with her. When she tells her mother that she's in love with a woman, the mother says that she won't tell Anna's father, underscoring the symbiotic tie that binds the two women.

Asked about her early movies, Akerman remarks, "When I did *Les Rendez-vous d'Anna*, which is a film I like, I felt I was not going forward. *Anna* said something else but it was the same approach to some extent (as *Jeanne Dielman*). Every movie must give me a different experience." *Toute une nuit* (1982), her first film of the eighties, marked a significant change. Shot at night, it follows a multitude of couples in the course of an evening on the town. Akerman explains, "It was a way to make a film without a lot of money, to work with more people, not so much a one-on-one situation. It is about hundreds of people having the same kind of love experience, as if to say, 'We're not unique anymore.' To some extent it's against romanticism. It's about an abyss that you fall into. *Toute* starts something, but you don't know exactly what."

It was a logical step for Akerman from the seemingly spontaneous movements of couples at play in *Toute une nuit* to the use of choreography and the musical in *Les années 80* and *Window Shopping* (1986). A cool unsentimentality underlies *Les années 80*, in which actors and actresses are shown auditioning for parts, reciting the same lines—love stories—over and over. But in the end, what was repetition is insouciantly pulled together as spectacle—an oddly comic musical. To hilarious effect, Akerman demonstrates how planned and directed both movies and life are. She herself appears—conducting a singer with forceful gestures and movements, an analogue to the director's role, which itself mimics the human desire for control.

Window Shopping is her full-tilt musical extravaganza, with Delphine Seyrig playing another Jeanne, this time a clothing-store owner in a French shopping mall. Although married, she falls in love with another man, while her son is in love with a girl in the beauty salon next door. They all sing their laments in stores meant to serve other kinds of consumers than those hungry for love. The mall is the stage on which Akerman parades not only love's familiar tales of hope and banality, but also the mundane anxieties of the shopkeeper. "I did the film," she says, "because my mother used to have a shop and she couldn't stand it. She said she felt like a whore in a window." Akerman's version of romance is mediated by irony and distance; as one character says at the end of the film, likening the lover's fickleness to the shopper's, "If you don't have that dress, take another one."

Akerman's newest film, *Histoires d'Amérique*, is her first feature in English, but it's an accented English, that of the Eastern European Jew who settled in America to escape persecution. "I have to say," Akerman tells me, "that my mother was in Auschwitz and she didn't say one word about it. This is important to the making of the film, although it is more like a series of imaginary memories." It's a film that "fills a gap, a kind of hole. It's about something unconscious." In a sense, Akerman is part of the community of contemporary European filmmakers, including Louis Malle, who are addressing the memory of the concentration camps. *Histoires d'Amérique* focuses on stories culled from letters written by the readers of *The Jewish Daily Forward*, a newspaper serving the immigrant population in New York at the beginning of the century (and still in existence). The setting for Akerman's film is Lower Manhattan. But rather than using crowded tenement apartments (like those made familiar by the documentary photographs of Lewis Hine), Akerman places her characters in deserted lots, at night, with trucks for props and isolated buildings as background. Homeless, they talk to the camera in monologues that describe separation from loved ones and birthplace. These accounts are framed by so-called Jewish jokes told by various twosomes. Deadpan vaudevillians come and go, reciting cryptic and funny stories that undercut the sadness of the personal histories.

"Everybody knows the jokes," Akerman says, "and I included them because it's a way for the Jews to put their own reality at a distance, in order to survive. If I chose to depict American Jews, it's because their uprooting was a bigger change of culture than if, for example, they had settled in Brussels. For the people living in Eastern Europe, it was more mythical to go to America. Their hopes were greater. But the film is not at all realistic. I show a lot of people because I don't want just one or two to represent all. The film is about a world that is slowly disappearing. I was using all those people as if they were ghosts reappearing in the night."

1989

7. Penis Story

It was a hot summer afternoon. I was walking on 57th Street. Between Sixth and Seventh Avenues, I saw a scholarly-looking man in his thirties — wire-rimmed glasses, stringy, longish hair, a bookbag. He was coming toward me, walking toward me as if he knew me. His bookbag hung down his chest, in a V, and settled there, like a pouch. He approached me intimately. New York summers are sultry.

Then he lifted his bookbag. He held his penis tightly in his hand, clutching it like a leash. When he saw me see it, saw my surprise or horror, his face lit up. With that indefinable but definitive look. I couldn't see myself, could only imagine my face.

I can picture a gallery of horrified women's faces. It's always bothered me, that satisfied look, his triumph, my foolishness, a jerk at the end of his chain. But life's filled with unimportant triumphs.

I continued walking, then stopped. It'd been a while since a man exposed himself to me. I realized that no one even mentioned it happening anymore. I began wondering if its time was over, if it was no longer a thrill, just a passing perverse gesture that will be recorded for history. Maybe tight pants killed it.

I remembered, with a weird, unexpected nostalgia, how many men I've seen expose themselves. There was a tall man on the 42nd Street subway station platform who jumped up and down, balletically, waving his penis. He choreographed his movements in time with the train, dancing close to the doors, leaping ecstatically one last time as the train pulled out.

There was a young Santa Claus at Macy's. I was about 18. On his break, he followed me when I went to make a phone call. He walked right up to the phone booth—he'd removed his beard but was in his Santa suit—and showed me his penis through the glass section of the door. Because he'd followed me, I was scared, and he was a Santa Claus in Macy's, which was a grotesque irony.

There was a little man in Paris, who was sitting on the Metro opposite a friend and me. She whispered: "Is he masturbating?" He was wearing forties pleated trousers with huge pockets. "Maybe he's scratching," I said, generously. As she and I stood up to leave, after a long, strangulated ride, the little man revealed his truth. He stared at us benignly and, with his thumb, lightly flicked his penis back and forth and from side to side. An unusual style or technique. Kind of like a puppet, I think now, in a Punch and Judy show.

There's been a range of expression, a variety, in the way men have exposed themselves over the years. Where'd it go? Movies, live entertainment, rock 'n' roll, show biz. I don't know.

I was still on 57th Street, astonished by the rare spectacle of a man having exposed himself at all. I consider: It's a relatively harmless attack these days. Compared with a stranger walking up to you, putting a gun to your head and blowing your brains out, raping you first, almost harmless. Everyone always said the guys who did that would never hurt you.

I turned to look for him and caught sight of him again. He was choosing his next female. He started walking toward her. He was moving his hand. He was ready to lift his bookbag.

But his name was called. Another woman called his name. A friend. She walked toward him. He was just able to hold his penis down with his bookbag. He smiled and managed to speak, obviously small talk. He rushed her, animated, awkward, and finally she said goodbye. A friend. The guy's not paranoid enough, or he really wants to be discovered. A friend at a time like this.

I followed him. I don't know how far I would've gone. But it was only around the corner. He had a job in a movie theater on 7th Avenue. He spoke familiarly to another man taking tickets in the booth. I watched him go inside, watched him take a seat in the booth, ready to sell tickets. I wanted to talk to him, didn't know what to say. It felt incomplete, a story without an end. I went home, by subway, and nothing happened.

1994

8. | Ugly

You can't leave anything behind that isn't acknowledged to be there or to have been there.

Racism, race-based thinking and attitudes are part not only of our lives and the history of this country, but also of the language, the American-English language, and of the habits, habitual language, of America. Since language both reflects and shapes experience, its usage is extremely important, urgent.

It's very hard to figure out how to write about race and writing. One way is the autobiographical route, to use one's self as example.

"I grew up in a supposedly integrated town. It wasn't. Our high school was a clearcut indicator of segregation, where the African-Americans and the Italian-Americans mostly took shop and were popular with the white, Jewish-American kids—or integrated—if they played football. The Jewish-Americans were on their way to college, whether they had the grades or not. Class, religion, and race all divided the school. It was my high school, Lawrence, that Jermaine Ewell attended. He was so badly beaten recently in a racial attack, he can no longer play football. That kind of attack didn't happen when I went there. But it isn't surprising to me that it happened now.

"Back then, we weren't supposed to be friends, to hang out together or date or have sex. I went to a few parties, though, where we all danced together. That was all right but dangerous if you danced too closely with a guy who was black or Catholic, Italian-American. I went into a deep depression in high school after the death of a friend, I withdrew from everything. I stopped going to parties.

"My gym teacher, who was a lesbian, which everyone knew though it was unspoken, wanted me to go out for track because I was a fast short-distance runner. But I didn't. Had I, I would have gotten to know better some of the African- and Italian-American girls. I actually liked gym better than the rest of school, with the exception of history and English classes, but I couldn't see myself being so visible, racing around the track, even for short distances. I was withdrawn and insecure. I wanted invisibility. And I would have been the sole white Jewish girl on the team. I only recently remembered that."

This is evidence of what I think is not uncommon experience for many northern white people—to grow up within forms of institutionalized racism and segregation. It wasn't called segregation.

Language is important. Racism and segregation were unnamed parts of the fabric of this northern suburban life, and it's hard to talk about, to find the best, most vital language to use, to write about what wasn't ever named or discussed.

I'm writing and remembering as a white person. I was not in the homes of the black students who may have complained, complained bitterly, to each other and their parents about this obvious, exclusionary system that disadvantaged them, and privileged us.

Then and now, racism usually was other people's doing—it happens in the South, for instance. Or, racism was a problem for black people. It was not a problem for white people: Racism deformed the lives of African-Americans, the objects of racism. But the subjects of racism—white people—who perpetrate it could avoid the terrible "problem" by not seeing it as a problem in themselves.

Theodor Adorno wrote in "Coming to Terms with the Past," an essay that addresses the German past, Nazism, and antisemitism:

> I also don't believe that too much is accomplished by social gatherings, encounters between Germans and young Israelis, and other such organized acts of friendship, however desirable this contact may be. For this sort of activity depends too much upon the assumption that anti-Semitism essentially has something to do with Jews and could be combated through an actual knowledge of Jews. In fact the genuine anti-Semite is much more defined by his utter incapacity for any kind of experience or his lack of receptivity. . . . So long as one wants to struggle against anti-Semitism within individual persons, one shouldn't expect too much from recourse to facts, for they'll often either not be admitted or be neutralized as exceptions. One should rather turn the argument toward the people whom one is addressing. It is they who should be made conscious of the mechanisms that provoke racial prejudice.[1]

Adorno writes about this as "turning toward the subject."

Back to autobiography:

"I remember the morning after Martin Luther King was assassinated. On that day, twenty-five years ago, the city was still, absolutely quiet, as quiet as a funeral home. On the subway—I was going to college—no one, black or white, looked at each other.

"I remember the morning after Howard Beach. I remember what the city felt like to me. It was horrifyingly like the morning after Martin Luther King was murdered. That night, after Howard Beach,

1. Theodor Adorno, "What Does Coming to Terms with the Past Mean?" in *Bitburg: In Moral and Political Perspective*, ed. Geoffrey H. Hartman (Bloomington, Indiana University Press: 1986), pp. 127–28.

I went to get Chinese food at a take-out restaurant on the corner, one block from home, and I was standing on line behind a young black man. There was some confusion about who was to be served next. I asked him: Excuse me, have they already taken your order? He didn't answer me. He wouldn't talk to me. I wasn't sure if he wasn't talking to me because of Howard Beach, because of his anger, or because he thought I was rude, trying to get ahead in the line, or what. I still don't know. There are many possible interpretations."

After Howard Beach—a community in Queens where a young black man was chased across a highway and murdered by two white men—I recognized, as if a curtain had been lifted from my eyes, some heavy social "fabric" I wasn't seeing through, and "saw" how severely and obdurately segregated and racist New York City was, was continuing to be, even after the Civil Rights movement and some gains. I don't think I was alone among white people.

There may not have been the same kind of citywide violent revulsion and rebellion that there was after the beating of Rodney King and the trial of the Los Angeles cops who did it and were acquitted. There was something much quieter. But in that dense quiet it could no longer be facilely said by whites that things were so different here from the South, because it was apparent that racism was not just prevalent, it was virulent, and it was living unchecked precisely because it was unnamed, because white people wanted to believe they lived in a liberal, tolerant city, and didn't want to see racism in their version of the city or themselves.

African-American New Yorkers knew and experienced the everyday, subtle and the extraordinary and violent racism. They knew that while racism had been different in the South, it was in place here, implicitly, as well as deeply, stealthily, and devastatingly. They were the objects of racism perpetrated by subjects who did not recognize their complicity, themselves.

("They knew..." It's a generalization that most African-American New Yorkers know, experience, this racism and live with discrimination. There may be some African-Americans who don't or haven't. I know there are women who say they have never felt discriminated against as women. Generalizing and generalizations are part of the problem of writing about anyone else's living in the world; my argument depends on the idea of a divide between blacks and whites experientially and structurally. But there are always exceptions, and exceptions are always interesting.)

What this apartheid—or separateness, apartness—between whites and blacks in experience means is that, among other things, there is also a gap in language, in understanding, in education, in every-thing. Because there is a gap in the language used to communicate and to articulate experience, and everything, there's a gap in writing, in what gets written and made.

Spike Lee's film *Do the Right Thing* was a direct, impassioned and brilliant response to Howard Beach. (My response was indirect, a concatenation of other determinants too—in part, it began with my novel *Motion Sickness*, but ultimately, it was more fully articulated in my novel *Cast in Doubt*, with the character Gwen, who is African-American.)

In *Do the Right Thing*, to my way of seeing, the Italian-American characters were better developed, more fully drawn than the African-American characters, with the exception of Spike Lee's character, but even his—this may be a question of acting—didn't have the range of Danny Aiello's and even John Turturro's, the announced racist. (In *Jungle Fever*, the Turturro character again is more fully realized than the character played by Wesley Snipes, who seemed to me less knowable, less developed psychologically.)

Here's the problem. Even Spike Lee, who can do, can make, so much, is hampered by the lack of well-drawn black screen charac-ters, but he's had a Scorsese and a Coppola, to name two, to bring him Italian-Americans. (As Adorno suggested, Lee addresses, through his representations of white people, the subjects of racism.)

Historically there have been relatively few black characters in movies who were protagonists, who had the main speaking parts. As maker, Spike Lee is at a disadvantage and at an advantage. The codes aren't in place. He has to figure them out, make it up, bed some, discard some. It's a raw, wild place to be.

In some of the movie's most powerful scenes, to represent the objects of racism, Lee pulled way back and, with a Brechtian arms-length distance, presented three black men sitting on the street, talking, commenting like a Greek chorus on the issues. (If I were a black writer, would I write "black" men?) The sidewalk characters are just "there," unexplained presences who explain. Lee eschewed "positive images" with them. Without a back story or explanation, they're open to interpretation, blank or "white" canvases. They can be projected onto easily, so Lee plants how they're seen in the eyes of the viewer, the subject, not in the objects on the screen.

Spike Lee is groping his way with his black characters. He's trying to invent a cinematic language, along with Julie Dash and many others. It's extremely exciting to be witnessing the birth — or renaissance — of this new cinema, to see it fight with and rely on, object to, bend and borrow genres and codes.

Similarly, there is a gap in what white northern people have produced in novels and short stories (and films) — an absence. It's a gap based on experience, usually segregated, and on the language which both reflects and shapes the experience. I look to Toni Morrison's resonant, suggestive thesis in *Playing in the Dark* that the Africanist presence is always there in books by white American writers, even when it's not explicit. There's no white without black, since the races are constructed always in relation to each other.

Sometimes in novels by white people there's an attempt to talk about relations between and with white and black people, but in a culture that has been and continues to be, in most ways, segregated, often these representations are awkward, thwarted, or simply stereotypes. There are few fictional models to use in the North other than the inner-city version — whites and blacks have contacts through the street, the dealer, the police, violence, etc. Gang warfare.

Alice Walker once wrote, in *Ms.* magazine, that she wanted white women to write about black people even if it was about "their maids." (I was struck by her demand when I read it in 1976.)

Dorothy Parker did write about a maid in her short story "Clothe the Naked," not "her maid" but a black woman who works in the homes of white women who are terrible to her. The story's told from Big Lannie's point of view. To a white person, like me, who had a home, which once had a maid, it's painful to read. I cried. (I showed it to a friend who's black; he didn't find it painful or moving.)

It's weird, isn't it, that there haven't been novels and stories by white people in the North that explicate the everyday racism that they were the subjects of. Most white people don't want to or haven't wanted to write about "their black maids." Writing it exposes a fact, a condition, which represents inequity, the very institutionalization of racism that wasn't named years ago.

In South Africa the most popular cartoon now, published in a liberal newspaper, is about a white woman and her housekeeper, "the black maid." It's upsetting to a lot of white people there, because it makes fun of and reveals certain liberal attitudes, the unspoken and supposedly nonvirulent forms of racism.

If fiction is important, it's important because it goes about constructing and representing in language and stories what is often unspoken or only imagined and fantasized. When written out, these unforgivable unspokens may expose wretched ambivalences and ambiguities, the many contradictions in our lives. Contrary to current opinion, what's "true" — meaningful — and significant doesn't reside only in the retelling of an actual event. While something may have actually happened, the way it's conceived or retold may be trivial or thin, "untrue" — stupid, false, silly, an idiotic, shallow or unprofound version or production, though based on "a true story." A "true" story can be a meaningless story in representation. An actual event doesn't "make" the film or story, the writer, artist, or filmmaker does. (Spike Lee's *Do the Right Thing* wasn't a documentary or a docudrama. It was a dramatic fiction based on events in Howard Beach.) Something doesn't have to have really happened to become the subject of a meaningful work.

Fiction is debased for its virtues, which are to contend and contest with so-called reality, to invent other possible realities, or stories, other ways to think, other outcomes, futures, pasts, to fantasize what's vile or beautiful or in-between, to let loose unconscious desires, to dig at boundaries, to foray into the uncontrollable, to poke at what's repressed, to try to unearth it—the unwanted, the awful, the ugly.

To put it simply, when I think about race and writing, and think about contemporary practice, I think there's going to have to be more honesty on the part of white people. If that happens in our writing, it will be ugly and offensive, the way racism is.

1994

9. Looking for Trouble
(or privileging the subtext)

I'm in upstate New York, looking out a window. The wind is blowing, whistling. The trees are bending. The leaves are dark shapes marking the grass and the asphalt roads. The world is shadowy, dappled and mottled, filled with special effects.

I stare out the window and ask myself, what was *The Bodyguard* about?

I know I'm not alone in holding garrulous, but mute conversations. I peer into my own one-way mirror. It makes the time pass.

The story of *The Bodyguard* goes like this: A mega pop star played by Whitney Houston is receiving death threats, and a private security guard played by Kevin Costner is hired to protect her. She does not know about the death threats, because they're intercepted by her "helpers." So first she resists Costner's help, but not his arms. Then she resists both for a while, but finally and climactically, she succumbs when she realizes the danger she's in. In short, she's pursued, he protects, she's saved by him, they fall in love. Dramatically, she leaves an airplane she's just boarded—he's standing on the tarmac—to run back to him. Her song *I Will Always Love You* (a Dolly Parton cover which, not inconsequentially, revives

Whitney Houston's "real" singing career) swells to a crescendo as they embrace.

Someone's playing a radio somewhere, the volume's just low enough so that I can't actually hear it, can't tell if it's talk radio or the news.

I sometimes fantasize what Hollywood producers say to each other about key moments in movies. I think about how much energy or interest is invested in bringing to the screen flagrantly whacked-out, oddly dubious work or deeply flawed curiosities. What about *The Bodyguard*? Money is just one motive in the mystery called the Hollywood movie. They could've made another movie.

The novelty of the country is distracting. It's supposed to be quiet, and it is at night, but during the day, when the trees blow crazily and you can see the shadows on the ground, it's noisy. People work with large machines that move dirt. They play their radios but not loudly enough. Country noise is different from the city's, where people run their engines in cars that idle, going nowhere fast, or raise their voices above the overamplified sounds of their CD players.

Once upon a time *The Bodyguard* might have been called an "interracial" movie romance. Now, I wonder, if this is an interracial movie romance when the race of its lovers/protagonists is *supposed* to be unimportant; or a new genre of interracial movie in which race is unimportant, or it's not an interracial genre movie because race is not important to the story. The racial difference of the protagonists isn't proposed—scripted—as an issue between them. This isn't meant to be the 90s version of "Look who's coming to dinner after the rock concert." But does this absence on a diegetic level mean anything or not? Or, is it absent? Is it being elided, ignored, or is it suppressed? Is it desirable not to notice or ignore? What is that desire about? And isn't what's suppressed bound to emerge somewhere?

There's a pool here, not far from my room. I wonder if there's a bodyguard, I mean, a lifeguard. They're summer's security guards, its vigilantes. Lifeguards at pools are different from the ones at the beach, who sit alone, perched on lofty platforms, their noses smeared with thick white cream. Zinc, I think.

In *The Bodyguard* race registers first implicitly, coded as cultural/
institutional difference: Houston is an entertainer and Costner the
law, and cleverly, when he "protects" her, he's "private law" —
unattached, a law unto himself, a freelancer. But pop stars, like
Whitney Houston, are above law anyway, any law. She doesn't
recognize his law initially, in any case.

High noon. The shadows are long.

When, in Miami, Houston finally permits Costner to rescue her,
to take her to a safe place, with her son and sister, where's the
mystery destination, the refuge? Costner's father's house, the family
home, in Vermont, Maine, or New Hampshire. From a terrace on
a hotel balcony in a hot climate, post chaotic pop concert, where
Houston's nearly been killed, the movie cuts to a winter wonderland,
to snowtopped mountains, to snow everywhere, to a blindingly
white and serene scene. A Hallmark Christmas card.

The Hallmark Card company has its home in Kansas. If my
view here were Kansas, everything would be flat, and there would
be hardly any trees for miles. Lots of corn and wheatfields. In the
city of Leavenworth, Kansas, not far from Kansas City and
Hallmark, there are five prisons—federal penitentiary (maximum
security), army (Fort Leavenworth), state, local, and women's. I
call it The Town Without Pity.

Costner leaps out of the van and runs to his father. Both men
turn to look at the three people Costner's brought with him. The
three are, by now, just standing there, dramatically dark or "black"
against the "white" snow. The father looks at the three who are
waiting patiently to be made welcome (a statement in itself):

> Father to Costner: "Are they all in trouble?"
> Costner to father: "Not all of them."

The dialogue cracks like the noise of a bat hitting a metatextual
home run. It shocks as if something were exposing itself, not a
penis, something more shocking, at least surprising. In its supposedly
non-race-based context, the exchange serves as a "white on black"
comment, a racial/racist sounding comment. But the weather (and

other conditions) isn't neutral: for one thing, it's on the ground, and it is the background against and on which the figures act. It's color-filled, coded. To quote Cornel West, suddenly it's clear that race matters. And, given the prevailing climate in the U.S., the antagonistic and distorted attitudes of most U.S. whites towards U.S. blacks, inscribed in country versus city, inner city especially, the lines signify a conversation about race(ial) matters. A couple of white guys are talking about blacks in the country.

What are those noises now? Clangs and then a humming. Red-faced men with walkie talkies are calling to each other and looking into the ground. Cars are rolling on gravel roads, birds are singing, chatting. I suspect the view outside this window would be remarkably the same every day. City streets are like rivers to me, in constant motion.

Did the movie's makers intend the dialogue merely to demonstrate a caring, older man, a good father available to everyone (almost impossible for a Hollywood movie not to be about fathers and masculinity these days)? The paternal can easily move into paternalism and, at the very least, those lines resound paternalistically. The scene that was contrived—that Christmas card—is a slice of a pie called white America. Its untouched and serene surface masks the pie, hides its crumbly apple filling, which is in trouble—and trouble, not just for the "others" who wait not so patiently for a fairer share of the national pie.

I watch a baby chipmunk run for cover under a dilapidated house.

In *The Bodyguard* a "real American" man—real Americans are not hyphenated Americans, they don't need adjectives—saves the African-American woman, and other people of color, not only from herself or themselves, but also, and more sinisterly, from each other. It was, pointedly, Houston's sister who hired the killer. Merely a plot point in the story, she's an undeveloped character who's supposed to be riven with envy of her sister. Costner rescues Houston from her sister's evildoing. It's all in keeping with the traditional Hollywood way, the Western (movie) way: a good white man will appear who will get the job done. He will save troubled, unprotected people, be a hero, take the country in hand, allow newcomers into (onto) the land. But even in the most slanted and egregiously anti-Indian Westerns, the Indians were acknowledged as Indians. There were recognized conflicts, battles, "between" white settlers and Indians, though the Indians were mostly disadvantaged in and by those narratives. In *The Bodyguard* the "disadvantaged" are further disadvantaged: underlying conflicts between blacks and whites are embedded in a narrative that builds on "trouble" subliminally.

I can't relax. I don't have a TV here but there are newspapers to read. The New York Times reports that girls in swimming pools are being attacked and fondled by groups of boys in a practice called "the whirlpool." The boys come at them in a swarm, a formation, and surround and attack. The lifeguards are outnumbered sometimes. One says: "We do our best. But we don't just jump in like that."

The Bodyguard is armed with powerful hooks: It's a desire machine producing not just romantic love but also a love that protects against danger, that makes one safe, that is itself safe. But that safety, its innocence, is questionable. Romance can function (it's labile), and desire can have more than one object, even contradictory objects. Romance is a good cover story, and romancing the "other" here obliterates the idea of an other, of the differences "between." *The Bodyguard* asserts that she—black, female—needs protection, but acts as if he—white, male—her protector, is neither dangerous to her, and others, nor in danger from himself and others like him.

There goes a jackhammer.

Racial conflict is the unmentionable, perilous secret of *The Bodyguard*, sitting at the back of the movie-bus, not supposed to be there, not supposed to be an issue. And it's easy to miss in all the garish confusion. Visually the movie is an accumulation of bright, brassy, and cluttered scenes, stuffed with action, lights, objects. Everything is happening, the scenes insist, as if all that glitters and glows, all that goes POP culture in the night, is meant not to be looked at or regarded seriously. Just window dressing, mere distraction.

There's a squirrel scooting up a tree. I once liked squirrels, but now I look at them and wonder if they're rabid. Two men have come along and are fixing something in the ground and talking about it. There's constant fixing going on in these parts, as they say.

A longer shot, another pet theory of mine, related but extrinsic to *The Bodyguard*'s narrative, is: It's likely that Costner was or is a Republican or a Reagan Democrat. In the movie Costner's character once worked in the elite corps that protects the President — Reagan — but was off duty the day that Reagan was shot. (He was getting married to the wrong woman.) Years have passed but Costner is still guiltstricken (suffering from an Oedipus complex). He thinks if he'd been there he could've saved Reagan, by which I take it to mean the father, the Republican party and the U.S. The party/country (and movie business) needs a hero like Reagan/Costner. *The Bodyguard* has a hero, who makes all the difference. Bases loaded home run. Costner scores, reaching home base on the backs of others who are playing without numbers on their shirts.

The wind has died down. The existence of satanic cults around these parts is exaggerated, I hear.

The Bodyguard is relentless in its mission to romance the nation, while *American Heart*, for instance, a movie about the state of the country, set in Seattle, has nearly the opposite (oppositional) drive. Jeff Bridges, toned, muscular, and tough-looking, plays a guy just out of jail, who tries to become a good father to his young, sadeyed Alain Delon-like son. But it's too late, and even an antihero with a tough body isn't viable, battling forces as big as and in tandem with psychological problems which challenge the probable success of individual acts of heroism. There are no heroes, there is an ex-prisoner who can't really get out of prison. The movie has a spare, quietly desperate look, its *mise-en-scènes* of devastation like the characters' faces and the face of the downcast (economically downturned) country.

A man has just walked by, drinking a beer. One night in a bar in New York, when I was going on about Coppola's *Dracula* being about Islam's challenge to Christianity and a new Crusades, the

West's terror of Islamic fundamentalism, and the "Muslim hordes infecting us" with bad (AIDS) blood, a woman said to me: "You privilege the subtext." I laughed and thought to myself, I suppose I do. Frothy, nasty, fascinating, entertaining, endlessly questionable—the subtext, that's where uncertainty rules uncertainly. Where the ambiguous never takes a vacation. Where never an innocent word can be heard (in my mind I'm hearing *Home, Home on the Range*). Always compelling, it's the parallel palace of the partly known, mostly unknown, unarticulated, indirect.

It rained yesterday. I didn't go outside all day. I'm the spy who didn't go out in the rain. Just a private eye in a public sphere. I want to cover the dirty laundry. Fran Lebowitz once wrote a column in *Interview* magazine entitled *I Cover the Waterfront*. My mother used to ask: Why look for trouble? A hardboiled kid, I answered, it looks for me.

In *A Few Good Men*, is director Rob Reiner contesting Oliver Stone's dominance in Hollywood, attempting to halt Stone as he advances to corner the market on movie manhood and patriotism? Is he telling Stone: You didn't have to have served in Vietnam to be a man or a good American? Reiner even quotes the crusty *Caine Mutiny Court Martial*, a trial drama, because where else try Stone but in a Hollywood court of law? After all, there are "a few good men" in Hollywood who are Oliver Stone's age and generation, like Rob Reiner, who did not fight in Vietnam.

Like President Clinton, who bombed Iraq again. Was it to boost Clinton's popularity or because Bush was bleating that if Clinton didn't avenge the attempt on his life, Clinton's presidency was finished? Or was it Colin Powell nudging Clinton: You give me another shot at Iraq: I'll give you gays in the military? All of the above?

And, what about *The Crying Game*? I heard some U.S. viewers adamantly refused to accept that Jaye Davidson was male, even after seeing the shot which panned down his body and revealed a penis, his. Does the movie ask: Is the body a foundation for anything? Doesn't it propose that love—desire—can conquer all and that it's always "natural" but not linked to the body? The object is always achieved, as well as the way to the object (even though the movie keeps insisting "it's in my nature," contradicting its own more interesting premises). Nature is itself the question in *The Crying Game*. And, interestingly, it was very popular here but not in Britain. Is that because, in the U.S., the focus of "trouble" was seen primarily as the sexed body, not as "the trouble" in the political body? Seen less as the politics of the IRA, Northern Ireland, and England than as the confusion and terrors of sexuality, of alienated bodies, of enforced fixed gendering? Its treatment of the terror one body can inflict upon another in service to a political body (because of having been born into one nation—"it's in my nature"—not another) could be observed with distance, from a safe distance. The protagonist's alienation from the IRA and his flight across the border were generally viewed as pre-text for the transvestite story, a different fight/borders crossing tale.

I like to go for walks on winding roads. I like not knowing what's behind the next bend. I feel content except when cars slow down and there's no one else around. Last week it stormed fiercely and three old trees came down, obstructing the road. Lightning had struck them and they lay there for a while. Fairly quickly they were removed, leaving no effects, no traces of the drama in the sky, which had flashed and raged indifferently, ferociously.

In the Line of Fire plays with some of the ideas in *The Bodyguard*, but flips them over and over like just so many pancakes. Clint Eastwood is in the Secret Service, a presidential bodyguard, who had been assigned to protect JFK on that awful Dallas day. Now someone else—John Malkovich—is gunning for the current president. The charged conversation between Malkovich and Eastwood is the subversive motor, the ailing American heart, of this movie: Why protect a bad president? Is America worth serving? What is heroism? Loyalty? Is there a good guy, a bad buy, and what makes the difference? How do public and private traumas intersect? The good and the bad—Eastwood and Malkovich—are a disillusioned, dialogical couple (of white guys), performing intimacy and identification in a verbal dance and duel choreographed by a relative of Raskolnikov. Since the Malkovich character has links to the government, he is a set of ironic, disturbing questions—about the price of protection, for one thing—which never surface in *The Bodyguard*. And, in another coupling—Eastwood's love affair with a female agent, Rene Russo—Eastwood continues his cinematic role: only male megastar in Hollywood tough enough, "masculine" enough, to afford to be feminist and even to be a feminist's enamored foil. In a scene only he could pull off, Eastwood offers to quit his job, for love of her.

The trees now remind me of totem poles, not telephone poles. Emile Durkheim theorized that the totem pole was the place around and at which society began; in a sense it was the social, the first instance of society. Movies are social instances, totemic, in this farfetched sense, a social place, a place to which one goes, a place about place. A place before one's eyes. Sometimes I am astonished at what happens before my eyes.

1993

10. Kiss of death

It's 2 a.m. *The Godfather* is on television. A few lines of dialogue, a couple of enigmatic or emphatic gestures—I'm hooked, riveted to the screen, awake until 5 a.m. I've seen it before. That doesn't matter.

Maybe it's Al Pacino's eyes, those sad, lustrous, and doglike eyes that later glow fierce and tough as his character metamorphoses, like coal under the earth's weight and pressure, from soft to hard. Mikey Corleone, sensible, quietly defiant, educated, who's not going to be his father's son, who's not going to enter the family's dirty business (families are dirty business), is transformed into Michael Corleone, an avenging angel/devil, who's driven to wreak justice/ havoc by the near-murder of his father, the God/father, Don Corleone, Marlon Brando.

Maybe it's the subtle movement of Brando's massive, padded cheeks and jaw. I may be secretly wishing that the wads of cotton Brando placed inside his mouth—to change his speech and appearance—will tumble out, that he'll begin to drool (he does drool a little during his death scene). I know the cotton won't pop out: I've seen this movie many times (we've all seen the movie before, it's always the same movie, or they're all the same movie).

It's not the wads of cotton. Between you and me, I'm easily seduced by appeals to undying loyalty. I'm in thrall to loyalty's sinister and ineluctable twin, betrayal. Womb to tomb, 'til death do us part, it's the love that dares to speak its name—family and father.

Fatal Talk

The Godfather is in the name of the father, the son, and the holy ghost. It's a love story, essentially without women, about men, a powerful Oedipal narrative in which if the sons stay close to, and respect, the Father, no one will get hurt. Oedipal fantasies dance from scene to scene, as one by one the sons obey or betray— in the name of the father-auguring salvation, the father's love, or retribution, death.

(The first movie I went to at night was a Russian version of *Romeo and Juliet*. My father took me. I don't remember how it happened that we went alone together, to this movie in particular. We sat close to the screen, the movie house was nearly empty, and both of us cried. I was seven or eight, if memory serves, and if it does, what does it serve?)

Outside, on the street, the dealers have vanished for the night and not even the usual drunks are sitting on the church steps, singing golden oldies. But I'm sure I'm not alone. I'm sure the city is filled with thousands of *Godfather*-watchers who, like me, experience any of its appearances as a second, third, or twentieth coming. I sway inwardly to the pulse of cinematic illusion, to the power of a family romance, to the narrative of nation and family, to the mystery of make-believe. Folded into its *mise-en-scène*, absorbed into its story, I listen as the men talk that fatal talk. Don Corleone huskily whispers to Michael, "Keep your friends close, but your enemies closer." (You don't have to be a Mafia capo to understand—any paranoid knows he's right.)

Along with its make-believe, what is it I make believe? (*The Godfather* encourages guilty confessions.) A wish for some ultimate authority to relieve me of the burden of conscience, the desire for an unshakeable tradition to which I would belong without question, a longing for an unambivalent relation to the family? My family. In *The Godfather*, of course, ambivalence threads its tortuous way through the projector, laid on to and into the picture as if it were its soundtrack.

Love is the background for hate, hate for love. They exist in immediate relationship to each other, almost as (gun) shot-counter-shot. In *The Godfather Part II*, Michael gives the order to have his brother Fredo, who betrayed him, and the family, killed. The scene of Fredo's death is perfect in its duality, its ambivalence. Coppola cuts from the lake, where Fredo and his assassin are fishing, to Michael standing behind a large plateglass window (he's got the big picture window, the screen, and like us he's also a spectator). In the boat, which is rocking gently, Fredo is praying, but we already know he prays when he fishes—but does he know he's about to be whacked? Cut to Michael at the window, waiting. Cut back to the boat and the lake. Then to Michael. Then to the lake, without the boat. A gunshot. Cut to Michael, his head drops down; to the boat. Fredo's body slumps down.

I can replay that scene again and again in my mind. And I've probably got it wrong, the sequence of shots is most likely different. Fredo's murder was set in motion earlier when Michael vowed to destroy all those who tried to have him killed. "In my *bedroom*, where my wife sleeps, where my children play." One night, with Michael in earshot, Fredo inadvertently (unconsciously) let slip that he was one of them, but Michael won't revenge himself until their mother dies. La Mamma Mia. Respect. Honor the Family. Even so, Michael gives the order—"He's your *brother*, Mikey, he's nothing without you"—to have Fredo killed. Murder in the family is a tragedy: killing someone else, the family business.

(As a child I loved watching the family's home movies and used to set up the projector and show them to myself over and over. There must be something appealing to me, let's face it, about a passionate family struggle that leads inevitably and tragically to death/murder. Which reminds me of *Rocco and His Brothers*. Is *The Godfather* the American *Rocco and His Brothers*? *Rocco* reminds me of *Romeo and Juliet*, which makes me think of doomed love, doomed families, my father and me . . .)

The first time I saw *The Godfather Part II*, it was playing on Broadway in Times Square. After Michael's wife (Diane Keaton) tells him that the miscarriage he thought she'd had was actually "an abortion, it was an abortion, Michael," he slaps her, hard. Many in the audience—the majority—cheered. I walked out.

Family Romance

The Godfather women, an oxymoron? They are mothers, sisters, daughters, wives, and mistresses, and nothing else. They are good or bad, saved or discarded. Michael's wife's challenge to his authority—in effect, patriarchy—is the abortion. He throws her out, and she becomes a pariah. Given life-in-patriarchy, is *The Godfather*, I wonder, as much a "woman's picture" as a "man's picture"?

That kiss of death. Maybe it's that kiss, that absolute articulation of ambivalence, that mortal meeting of mouths, of Eros and Thanatos, that I relish most. What a romance. *Famille fatale.*

The Godfather Part II is on tomorrow night. I'll try to tape it. My obsession gobbles time (in a way, obsession is about time, it uses and makes nothing of time). The thrill is losing myself in it again and again and again. My history in its version of History (the nation's history as one immigrant family's story: *The Godfather* supplies the past also to render its own internal authenticity). My family romance in its Family Romance (my mother warned, "The only people you can count on are your sisters"). Were I still a child (I suppose I am, in a way), I might be hoping that in *The Godfather*'s next coming, there'd be a happy ending.

1992

11. Ray Charles

It's hard to know what's an influence. The indirect compels me more than the direct; and what I can't see or decide about is achingly interesting. The unconscious does fine, dirty work. Can anyone determine influence exactly, because by the time you can say, I was influenced by this, you're already in motion, propelled by other, unknown forces. But you don't know where you're going, really, or why you focus where you do. What you call an influence may be a marker of what you think you think, more a symptom, or a hope, than an influence.

I can build a set, an erector set, of influences now, retrospectively—my self as a menu, a museum, a trailer for a movie, or a music store in a shopping mall. I can name books, movies, relatives, teachers, songs, friends, conversations, bars, weird, even articulated moments, that have passed, or have been passed through, or that I passed by, and call them influences.

When I think about poems, I think about rhythms and sound, intensity, precision, distillation, strong words that dance to an internal beat. So if I return to "first things," and I can't, because I can't repeat the past, I'd say the poems that moved me, turned me around first, were Ray Charles's songs.

Like "What'd I Say." Its long, wordless intro, like breath itself, breaks into: "Hey, Mama, don't you treat me wrong./ Come and love your daddy all night long./ . . . See the girl with the red dress on,/ she can do the birdland all night long./ . . . Tell me what'd I say, tell me what'd I say right now/ tell me what'd I say/Tell me what'd I say right now./ And I want to know./ And I want to know right now."

What did I know, at 10, about doing the birdland all night long? Wanted, hoped to know. Did I love his bittersweet lover's doubt? His anxious repetitions? Did I appreciate his desire to know? "I want to know."

Maybe I heard in Ray's voice, discovered in his passionate language, possibility, dimension, measure. His big, warm, intelligent sound was an embrace I'd never had; it held me around. His words partnered his rhythms. Lean language, fat sound. I thought I understood the words, even if I didn't.

Ray's singing, and playing the piano, the horns are punctuating and pushing, the Raeletts are backing him up, their higher, cooing tones full of pleasure, and I'm dancing around in the living room with my friend Jill. I'm listening hard. I hear how intense a word can be, just one word, then how powerful that word is next to others. Everything's driven by rhythm, words come in cadences, everything counts, has a count. The words hit on time, beat along with his circumspect, audaciously discreet piano. His canny emphasis and phrasing, his interpretations, make meaning wild. And then there's always something in his voice that spreads over the beat, as if the human voice is excessive, as if it always must exceed itself, life itself. There's too much in it. But Ray's the soul of discretion. What he leaves out is as close to intention as anyone gets.

1994

12. What Are Values?

"What Are Values?" Spectacolor Big Board, Times Square, New York, 1987, project sponsored by the Public Art Fund. Photo credit: Andrew Hill

13. Hole Story

Like other objects remembered from childhood, a book is alive, absolute, vague and partial. Dreamlike, memory reassembles (and resembles) the past, a scene or a moment, and always in pieces: a sound, smell, color, shape. The script I write and cast as Memory is almost intangible and unfailingly incomplete. I turn and look at my bookshelves. There's a snapshot of my mother, my sister, and me, I'm the infant in the baby carriage. I keep a memory: I'm little, with my mother, walking over a footbridge; there's another woman and a baby carriage. Something disturbing happens. My mother doesn't remember the scene. She thinks I dreamed it. Is the picture what I remember?

When I was about five I read a seemingly simple tale that was impossible for me to grasp. A little girl has a blanket. The blanket gets a hole. The little girl wants to get rid of the hole so she cuts it out. The hole gets bigger, and she cuts that out. She cuts and cuts and finally the blanket disappears.

I read the story over and again, as if it might change, and at its new end explanation would erupt from its pages. But the story's dire conclusion—the blanket disappears—left me trying to understand why it made sense and didn't make sense. Why couldn't she cut out the hole? The mysterious effect of reading, the immense undecidability of meaning, all this was contained in a book whose title, author and illustrator I can't remember. And no one's ever heard of it. The book is like a memory whose status as an object is in question.

But I remember reading it on my bed, and on the floor of the bedroom I shared with one of my sisters, and sitting in a big chair, in a room whose walls were papered brown, with little blue and yellow flowers. I didn't like brown. Was the radio on? Was I aware of girls and holes? What am I making up?

Years later I wrote a novel in which a character reads the blanket story. By incorporating the lost book into "my" book I found a way to restore it to some kind of existence outside, and yet within, "me." Now as I write about it again the blanket story gains significance and structure, becomes a private myth in my scripted childhood, overwhelming everything else, much as the hole consumed the blanket.

1992

14. Boots and Remorse

This story has a beginning. I have a friend named Amy who, years ago, had seven cats. Not only did she have seven cats, but at the time she also fed strays. I remember her telling me about one cat who lived behind a wall. She would leave food for it in front of a slit in the wall, a hole, and somehow, in the miraculous way cats have, the cat would squeeze through the hole and eat the cat food. Every night Amy made her rounds with cans of cat food, a can opener, and water too, and she would deposit everything at the appropriate though improbable homes and imperceptible feeding holes.

Our family had a cat. Her name was Griselda, and she was a brilliant calico. I didn't know, for example, that you weren't supposed to train cats to sit up and beg, or crawl, but because I was only five and Griselda was compassionate, she let me teach her. She also used to imitate my mother and wear her lipstick, rubbing her thin cat lips on an uncovered lipstick tube, or, uncatlike, she'd only give birth if my mother was in attendance, assisting. When my mother visited friends, Griselda would wait outside their houses, ready to walk her home. The Griselda tale had a sad end, one that still infuriates everyone in my family; I don't want to write it.

I loved cats, but I didn't have one. Amy wanted me to adopt one of the strays she fed. I was resistant, undecided, and guilty, since every night she'd go out and care for animals I supposedly loved but did not provide a home for. With a lot of excitement Amy announced that she had a cat for me, one she'd been feeding since he was born. She said he was the perfect cat for me and she continued: He is the most handsome cat I have ever seen. And the smartest. I told Amy I'd consider him. I was tempted by her high praise, which I never considered might be hyperbolic. It came from someone who'd seen many cats and had many of her own. The smartest. The most handsome.

One night I returned home to find a message from Amy on my answering machine: I've trapped your cat with turkey. I lured him into the cat carrying case and he's in my hallway, I can't bring him into my loft because of the other cats. Call me as soon as you get home, no matter what time it is.

I called her and went right over. In the hall Amy opened a large cat carrying case—she had several that were big enough to take two or more cats in case of fire. A skinny black and white cat with a pink nose and long face emerged. He was terrified, dirty, and scrawny, and he was ugly. Anyway I thought he was ugly, and I don't like cats with pink noses, but there Amy was, standing next to me, and she thought he was handsome. I couldn't say anything. We were in a sense both trapped in a sort of arranged marriage. I told Amy I liked him. He became my cat. I named him Boots because of his best feature, his white paws.

Amy says that it didn't happen this way. She says, first, she brought me to the car under which Boots lived, to view him, and then, when he came out, terrified, scrawny, and dirty, and in my eyes ugly, I was unenthusiastic. But this, Amy explains now, did not deter her; that is, she knew I didn't want Boots, but she trapped him anyway.

*

Boots and I reached my loft, or office. I was living on the sixteenth floor of an office building on John Street. We residentials were illegal tenants, sharing the building strangely with jewelers and other businesses forced to tolerate us. As soon as I opened the cat carrying case, Boots jumped out and ran crazily around the room until he found a hiding place. He disappeared for at least a week. I put food out and left the room, and when I returned, it would have been eaten, but I never saw him. It was as if he weren't there. I hated him but he was my cat.

It was the end of summer. I was working at a job that I also hated. As I was addressing envelopes for a bulk mailing, I realized with a tremendous shock that I had left my windows open, wide open, and that Boots, the cat I hated and had never even petted, that Boots might leap out and fall sixteen stories and land splat on the street, and die. And it would be my fault. Melancholic, I began to think about Boots, what a nice cat he was, how scared he was and what a terrible person I was, so unfeeling, ruled by an aesthetic that excluded pink noses and so on. I thought I would die until I returned home. Finally, breathlessly, I did. I looked out the windows and down and I looked all around the room and even behind the refrigerator. There he was. My Boots, alive. How I loved him. He didn't become a lap cat or even an affectionate animal, but he started to come around, and when David, a musician, moved in with me, Boots took to him.

David says that I did not find Boots immediately. He says that I arrived home in a panic, and when I couldn't find Boots anywhere, I telephoned Amy. She advised me to move the refrigerator. And there he was.

Boots liked David, who was and is much more patient than I. David taught him how to play, for instance. Life went on, and Boots began to sleep under the covers next to David, which for a cat shows trust. Boots loved David; I don't think he ever forgave me for my initial lack of interest.

There were many reasons he might have had for not forgiving me. One night I came home drunk. I don't actually remember doing it, but I found another black and white cat on the street, picked him up, carried him home, and he terrorized Boots. By the time David returned—which was and is usually late, musician time—I was asleep, dead to everything. The cats were engaged in territorial combat, and they kept David up all night. It must have been pretty strange for David, two black and white cats where there had been just one, mirror images screaming and racing around the apartment. We gave the cat away the next day and I don't remember exactly how or to whom.

David says that he did not stay up all night. He says he woke me right away and forced me to take the other cat downstairs, to the street, where I'd found it.

Sheila lived on the sixteenth floor too—she had a cat named Ocean—and we were making a film together. After five years, we were finally editing the film. By then Sheila had moved away and David and I had also moved, with Boots, to East Tenth Street. The first night in our new apartment Boots was so terrified that he didn't come out from under the blankets. He also didn't move for the next day or two. He stayed absolutely still while the neighbors downstairs yelled murderously at each other.

Boots adjusted gradually to his new home. The more I think about him, the more I realize how insecure and disturbed he was. Which makes the story I'm telling even more heartbreaking and me even more horrible. But I'll go on.

Sheila and I were editing our movie in an office on John Street, where we'd once lived, and one day, before starting to work, we went to Chinatown for dim sum. Leaving the restaurant, we encountered a black and white cat who came out from under a parked car and followed us. He was so short and stocky, he looked no more than ten months old, a kitten, I thought. Sheila said we had to rescue him. She grabbed the cat, which was easy—he didn't resist, he wanted to go with us—and carried him wrapped in her jacket all the way back to the editing room. Once we were there and settled into our editing positions, Sheila at the controls, me behind her in another chair, the cat settled into his position on my lap. He was more than a lap cat, he was a rug, since he didn't so much sit on my lap as cling to it.

I knew I had to have him and so I went home that night and began telling David about the new cat and how adorable he was and how we had to have him and how Boots would one day adapt to him and how he would like a friend and how we couldn't put him back on the street, how cruel that was, and how I loved him. David was adamant. No, never, one cat, that's all, not another cat, you can't do this to Boots. I already knew Boots didn't want a companion since he didn't like company, and scarcely wanted to be with us—or with me, anyway.

I had to have the new cat. Every night, after working in the editing room where the little stocky fellow was alternately loving and angry, but always clinging and needy, I pleaded with David. I did this for a month until David, enervated and exhausted with saying no, reluctantly agreed. He resigned himself to it, but he was, and remained, against the idea. It was greater than stubbornness. David identified with Boots. It was as if I were bringing a new man, a lover, into our home. This made David and Boots even closer.

David says he never agreed. He says that his music workshop teacher died around this time and he was depressed, in mourning. He says I took advantage of his weakness.

I brought the new cat home and named him Tuba after the latest instrument David was playing. I suppose I was hoping to inveigle the cat Tuba into David's musician heart just through its name, a cheap shot which did not melt David. He viewed Tuba as an interloper and a threat, to Boots and to himself. I was the engineer, the agent, of this destruction; I was breaking up our home and staying in it. If she could do this, I felt David felt, she could do anything. David paid even more attention to Boots to compensate for my sin. He hardly even looked at Tuba and almost never petted him.

The most important thing, though, was how Boots reacted to and treated Tuba, how they got along. They fought, of course, all cats fight with each other initially. And although Boots was furious, attacking, and ferocious, Tuba, from the very beginning, was imperturbable, indifferent, and fearless. Tuba's ears were notched, marked by many battles; he had a hairless scar on his thigh from a car accident or a devastating and calamitous catfight. He was, let's say, streetwise and cocky. Tuba did not seem to have any worries about Boots, the older, much bigger cat whose territory he was invading. This must have further disheartened Boots, who was, as I've already described, insecure, paranoid, and long-suffering.

On Tuba's first night with us, Boots slept, as usual, under the covers next to David. I awoke to discover Tuba sleeping snuggled into the crook of my arm, with his head on my shoulder. From the start, Tuba wasn't afraid to be on the bed even though it was Boots's place. In cat parlance, I believe we humans were to Boots the dominant cats, especially since we provided food for him, but Tuba was neither wary of us nor concerned about Boots. He assumed his place immediately. After a while, Tuba liked to sleep on top of Boots as he lay under the covers. What Boots made of that I don't know. He may have been indignant.

Tuba annoyed Boots. The younger cat wanted to play with him and liked to tease him. No matter how many times Boots let Tuba know he wasn't interested, that he didn't like him or want to play, Tuba insisted. He was unstoppable. Jauntily, insouciantly, Tuba always came back for more. Unlike Boots, Tuba is sure of himself. Overall, Boots was, I think, immune to Tuba's charm.

Four years passed. Boots was becoming stranger and stranger; I now know this in retrospect. It's that imperceptible thing, like the slits in walls cats can squeeze through, how you can live with someone, a friend, a lover, a cat, and not recognize, because they're so close, or that's what one tells oneself, because one has a stake in not knowing, most likely, not recognize what's happening to that cat, that lover, that friend.

More and more, strange noises disturbed Boots. Increasingly, strangers coming into the house angered him. Everything upset him. I didn't put it all, pull it all, together. There were incidents that seemed isolated, at first. My friend Diane came over to give me a shiatsu massage; Boots went for her legs. She was shaken. I played it down. Boots even went for David's legs once, but not badly. I became wary about having friends over because I didn't know what Boots would do. (It's a strange worry: Should I ask so-and-so over; what if Boots attacks?) Incidents were building one on top of the other, but then Boots would be fine for days on end. So I'd push away the bad event, already a memory, and decide it was an anomaly after all. Then, suddenly, he'd get weird or crazy again. It was like having a mad dog in the house except it was a cat. *Chat lunatique.* Boots was changing for the worse, and life with him was extreme and unpleasant in the extreme, at least for me—he and David had a good relationship still, which was not easy to bear. I didn't know what was happening to Boots, what to name it, or what to do about him, and because I didn't I tried not to think about it. Boots had his good days.

David reminds me that when his friend Wayne, another musician, visited, Boots jumped up into the cupboard and, from all the many jars and cans, threw down a can of his cat food. Wayne thought Boots was a genius. David led Wayne to believe he did too.

One Sunday the doorbell rang. It was the upstairs neighbor. She needed something. I walked away to get it but when I walked back, to give it to her, Boots leaped out and dug all his claws into my left calf. He hung onto and clung to my bare leg, with his claws, with an insane ferocity. The neighbor stood and stared as I tore him off me. I watched tissue oozing from the bloody holes dug deep in my leg. All the fur on Boots's body stood out. He seemed double his size. I poured hydrogen peroxide on my calf and found Band-Aids. I had been intending to meet my friend Craig for dinner. I wanted to cancel but Craig wasn't well, had AIDS, and I didn't think I could cancel because of my cat's attacking me.

It sounded an unlikely, insignificant, and bizarre excuse.

At the restaurant my calf started to swell and since I tend to imagine the worst, not unlike Boots, I suppose, I was distracted and worried, and also feeling immensely stupid, almost feeble-minded. Luckily a doctor Craig knew was in the restaurant and I asked him if I had to get a shot, and he said I didn't, unless it looked very bad the next day. I now can't remember if I went for a shot. I still have small depressions in my calf where Boots's claws dug in, though.

Before Craig died in 1990, he had a cat for about a year. Craig discovered the cat on a rainy, miserable day, lying in a box in a garbage can in front of the brownstone where he lived. Craig wasn't sure if she was dead or not, and he asked me to go downstairs and see if she was still lying there. I carried her from the garbage pail up five flights of stairs to his apartment. She moved, was alive, so I brought her to a vet near Craig, for a checkup and shots. Craig named her Miss Kitty after the woman in "Gunsmoke."

In the beginning Craig was anxious about whether Miss Kitty was happy or not. I think she was. She rewarded Craig with affection and devotion, spending most of her time lying next to him on his bed. Craig was less lonely because of her. Toward the end he couldn't care for her anymore, and I helped find her a home. That was a sad story too. Craig never knew it didn't work out exactly as planned, but Miss Kitty at least did find a home, even if it wasn't the intended one.

Now that Boots had attacked me, badly, something had to be done. It was obvious. Boots was watching my every move. The farther from the bed I walked, the more alarmed Boots became. He would follow me, stalk me, his fur sticking out from his body. He'd walk very close to my legs. I was afraid, and to be afraid of a domestic animal is disorienting. First of all, you feel insane being terrified of your pet and everyone else finds it funny. Even I thought it was funny in a way. Tuba noticed nothing, I think.

I telephoned the vet I trusted—she had discovered what four

others had not: Tuba had an obstruction that was causing his constipation, which meant he had to eat baby food mixed with fiber softener for the rest of his life. I described Boots's behavior. She said that some people had had success with a pet therapist, whose number she gave me. I assumed a pet therapist was an animal trainer, a behavior-modification trainer. I made an appointment.

Boots behaved himself for days before the appointment and I began to think it was unnecessary. But the doorbell rang at 10 a.m. as planned. I went downstairs to let the pet therapist in. She was wearing a yellow slicker and hat, had come on a bike, and was very short, like an elf.

She and I walked the four flights to my door and when I opened it, Boots assumed an attack position not ten feet from us. He wasn't going to let her in. It was uncanny. He'd never done this before; I'm sure he knew why she was there. For about ten minutes she stood in the doorway, making cutchy-cutchy-coo noises to Bootsy-wootsy. Boots, his fur all fluffed out, was unmoved. She said again and again, He wants to attack. Yes, I said.

David was in the shower; he was leaving for a tour of Germany later that day. Our apartment is a large railroad, and the only room with a door is the bathroom. When the shower water stopped running, the pet therapist said: Get David to distract Boots, to call him, and then have David put him in the bathroom and shut the door. David distracted Boots, put him in the bathroom, shut the door, and she was able to enter our apartment. We sat down at the kitchen table while Boots meowed in the bathroom. David packed.

First the pet therapist instructed me to record on audiotape what was spoken in the session. In addition she asked me to play a tape of Keith Jarrett-like music which she had brought, so that the music would also be recorded as background to her voice. All of this I did.

Then she opened her writing pad and inquired about Boots's history. I was in analysis at the time and not unfamiliar with the kinds of questions she was asking, although, with the putative patient locked in the bathroom, this was irregular. I was impatient but trying hard to take her and the process seriously since this might be Boots's only chance.

I narrated the sad story of Boots's life, where he was born, how Amy fed and then trapped him, that he was paranoid, that I was the one who brought Tuba in, that Boots loved David more than me, and on and on. I kept expecting that soon she would open the bathroom door and do something with Boots, begin to retrain him or talk to him at least. The more I related to her—Boots didn't trust me, I had betrayed him—the more I felt I had destroyed Boots, just as David told me I would. I spoke for about twenty minutes, answering all her questions to the best of my ability. Then she said that she was going to write up her assessment and, while she did, I could read an article about her. It was in *The New Yorker*, a Talk of the Town column. Apparently she'd had some success with a large, unhappy gray cat and appeared to have been taken seriously by several of her clients. By the time I finished reading the favorable, only mildly ironic story, the pet therapist had finished her analysis of Boots.

She looked penetratingly, steadily, into my eyes. Gravely she explained that Boots was suffering from "kitten deprivation syndrome." Then she gave me instructions. I was to play the tape of her voice for Boots three times a day, to calm him. Since Boots loved David, she asked if David would say something to Boots on the tape, a message Boots could listen to so that he would know David was coming back. David was still packing, dressed in his terry cloth robe; I brought him to his studio area, where she asked him to record his personal message to Boots. I believe he said, with an aggrieved smile: Hey, Boots, I'll see you later, man.

She wanted me to call her in a few days. Then she left. But before she left I paid her. Eighty dollars. Everyone always wants to know that. To me that was insignificant, the least of it. I telephoned the vet and complained. I never thought that when the vet said "pet therapist" she meant that. The vet suggested Valium and having Boots's front claws removed. I agreed. The alternative was worse.

Some time after that, Boots went for my legs again and even without his front claws, he ripped the skin. And he received a greeting card from the pet therapist, addressed to "Sir Boots Tillman." The card had a picture of a happy cat on the cover. On the inside, in a scrawl, she wrote her message: "Dear Sir Boots, Don't worry, everything's going to be all right. Signed, Sunny Blue the Wizard."

David left again for a tour of Canada, just a weekend, but I would have to be alone with Boots. Boots and Tuba. Tuba was hardly a comfort when he was one of the reasons Boots hated me.

By the way, during this period of extreme desperation, and out of curiosity as much as anything else, I did once play the pet therapist's tape for Boots, who, of course, ignored it. I also gave him Valium and took some myself.

While David was out of town, late on the Saturday night of a Fourth of July weekend filled with loud bangs and blasts, Boots jumped up onto the kitchen table. All his hair fluffed out and his head rolled from side to side on his neck. His eyes, as big and round as headlights, followed me like radar. It was something like the effect in *The Exorcist* when Linda Blair's head spun around. Boots was bigger than ever. Somehow I found the courage to grab him by the neck, throw him into the bathroom, and close the door. Boots hated the bathroom because that was his room for punishment, for isolation. But I was afraid to sleep with him near me. I thought he might go for my eyes. I'd seen that in a movie.

I awoke in the middle of the night to find Boots sleeping not on the bed beside me but on the floor next to the bed. That was startling. First of all, how had he gotten out of the bathroom?

The night before I had taken the precaution of bringing his cat carrier down, just in case. I decided to get out of bed, to move very slowly, not to alarm Boots, and walk to it. I wanted to shove Boots into it and keep him there, locked inside, until David came home. As I walked toward the carrier, Boots began stalking me, his fur thickening and fluffing. I grabbed him by the scruff of his neck and stuffed him into the case. I did this very quickly, in one motion, as if I had trained for it. Then, terrified, I telephoned David in Canada and demanded that as soon as he returned he take Boots to the animal hospital, to have him killed. I could write, to have him put to sleep, but killed is right. I would keep Boots in his case until then.

The next night, Sunday, David arrived home. It was late. He put his suitcase and bass down and with barely any words between us, he lifted the cat case and left. He was gone about two hours and when he returned, without Boots, I cried. I sobbed, I think. David had held Boots while the doctor injected him. David said Boots's eyes rolled back into his head. He died instantly.

David says it didn't happen this way. He says that he came home early on Sunday morning, but I was out of town, on Long Island for the Fourth of July. He took Boots out of the case and they spent a relaxed and happy day together. When I arrived home late, and saw Boots out of his carrying case, I insisted that David take him, right then and there, to be killed. Murderer, David says now, half-seriously.

Craig died early on the morning of a Fourth of July two years later. My mother wanted me to incorporate all her Griselda stories into my Boots story. I told her I might.

In case I ever forget, there are photographs of Boots and Tuba sitting next to each other. The sun is shining brightly on them, their bodies casting long shadows on the floor. Both cats are looking at the camera, serenely, as if posing for a formal portrait. They seem peaceful, even content. They were known to groom each other on occasion and even to nap next to each other, but they always fought. Boots may have been going senile. He may have had a brain tumor. There are explanations, one can look for and find explanations, but I don't know. I can't explain what happened.

1994

15. Criminal Love

I like the fantasy of falling in love. I love the feeling of being in love, succumbing to pleasure, being oblivious and indifferent to everything but love's craziness. I want to experience ecstasy, to be blinded to life's ordinary cruelties and anxieties. I want to forget myself and be myself extremely. I want passion to reign as delicious dictator. I want to make love perfectly. I want to be made love to exquisitely. Sex is the body's only relief for this wild love. I want to run riot, go out of control. In love, I become the agent of my own submission. In love, I suffer from a delusion, a magnificent obsession.

My occasional desires and fantasies are not unusual and, in an important sense, not even entirely my own or of my own invention. I plunder a set of existing concepts designed by and for desirous human beings. Like others I'm suffused with longings and drives. At my imaginary center there's emptiness. I'm not whole or wholesome. I need something all the time. Emptiness propels me to fill myself up. My search for comfort, warmth, pleasure, and well being sends me on a relentless journey. Sex and love dangle promise. They beckon me to rest in their arms.

Longing, blindness, oblivion, passion—the language of love—
describe an extraordinary condition that's common; the words are
common too. Most of us learn the language early, become
acquainted with the concepts. We expect one day to live the fantasy,
talk the talk. More than that, we want it directed to us—"I want
you, you drive me wild." Love is the happily disorienting eruption
and interruption in daily life. If it doesn't happen, we wonder if
we missed our escape from the dreariness and difficulties of life.

I turn on the TV. I lie on my bed in front of the set. With the
remote control in my hand, I coolly change channels. Ads for
telephone companies offering faster and cheaper connections
between lovers and friends sometimes make me cry. Turning to
Court TV, I watch a morning in the trial of *The State v. O.J.
Simpson*. O.J. Simpson, a magnificent athlete, was a hero to
millions. Now he's in jail, on trial for the murders of his ex-wife,
Nicole Brown, and her friend, Ronald Goldman. The litany goes:
He's black, she was white. He's rich, famous, handsome. He beat
her. He had everything. Black, he can't get justice. He's being tried
by the media. Or, famous and rich, he can buy justice. Even the
networks preempt some of their regular daytime programs to cover
the trial—to the horror, perhaps, or incredulity of the rest of the
world.

I can't stop watching. Eros and Thanatos are dueling on
television. Fascinated, I'm a voyeur in spite of myself. The courtroom
has transformed into a theater of tragic and comic possibilities, a
site of truths and falsehoods. The irresistible heart of this weird
show is the stuff of fairy tales and myth—the reversal of fortune.
A hero becomes a scoundrel, a great love turns to violence and
death, and a family is destroyed. Lives are ended, or they are changed
forever.

I turn the sound down and make myself a cup of tea. Love can
be desperate, a kind of madness, deranging. In its name, one
voluntarily commits oneself to mayhem. A relationship that may
have begun gently, with compassion and tenderness, often ends in
emotional violence. Or physical violence. Crimes of passion. Some
don't call this love. Some say love precludes violence. Some like

analyst Melanie Klein think that love is amibivalent, that hate is part of love. The two terms certainly can convert into one another. Compulsion for the loved one slides grimly and easily into repulsion.

I'm hungry for something sweet but resist it. When oblivious love calls, it urges, Lose Yourself. Whether for punk icons Sid Vicious and Nancy Spungeon or opera's Tristan and Isolde, the terms of undying romantic love are extreme. Stringent, informal laws encourage mutual self destruction or sacrifice. Enticing and exacting, enduring love promises intense excitement, or danger, but a reason to live. It can happen only if you obey the rules and lose a part of yourself to your lover.

I pour more tea, but avoid the cookies. There has to be some frustration. Love must be frustrated. Release is nothing without it. It's not just sexual release but the satisfaction of having finally discovered one's "true" self. But this is a melancholy pursuit. The stricken lover needs to find an other, to be fulfilled, or is doomed to a kind of half-personhood. The vulnerable lover may ultimately be denied, even denigrated. One's love may be rejected.

I eat an orange. I remember the way he looked at me. It was a strong drug. That's what first made me want him, his wanting me. I was excited by his desire, and his desire was uncontrollable, beyond my control. Then it started to control me. Inevitably he let me down. When he finally had what he wanted, he no longer wanted it. His was a perverse response, usual to love.

I brush my hair. That's the trouble with love. You can't control it. You can't control yourself. You put perfume behind your ears or slap aftershave on your face. You practice an enigmatic smile or try not to frown. But nothing you do will ever guarantee that he or she will love you. Or desire you forever or with abandon. Nothing.

I rinse my cup. Every time I fell in love, I fell in love thinking I would not fall in love the way I did the time before. Then I did. It's a kind of fidelity to the idea of love itself.

The early days are so similar, it's hard to tell one affair from the other. We either fell deeper in love or became disillusioned. The man was depressed, maybe mean. Or he was still secretly in love with the woman before. He was boring. We didn't want the same thing, but didn't really know what that was. The sex was nothing. When a love affair goes sour, or when it just cools down, the emptiness returns, and in its place is anger or despair, indifference or despondency.

I hate the aftermath. There are months of depression, of lying in bed, of crying in bed. Sometimes there's fury. What you needed to make you happy has been stolen from you. Love becomes a criminal. You rage against your fate. You relive a single, dark moment when all was lost. Hope died when love revealed its nasty side. Now dead love is hideous inside you, ugly. It might eat you alive. Unwanted lust feels palpable, impossible. It's an absence, a negation.

I put on my coat. I need some air and walk downstairs to the street. It doesn't have to be this way, I keep thinking. One doesn't have to fall in love like this. Yet the way romantic love has been constructed must correspond to the drives and instincts that Freud theorized about. We're born wanting and needing. Everyone wants. Why else would this peculiar fantasy of fulfillment endure so tenaciously, grip us so fiercely?

I look at sexy movie posters and graffiti painted on the walls. I watch men and women look at each other. Some eye each other indirectly. Some shoot hard glances. Some stare, as if saying, Fall in love with me now. Some look knowingly at the other, then walk past quickly.

I study two dogs, who are sniffing each other. The big dog circles the rear end of the little dog. Dog love and sex seems direct, obvious. It's harder to tell with people. Body language is indicative but often inconclusive. The body can't be read like a book. Bodies lie too. I've been with lying bodies. Mine has lied.

I stop at a newsstand. The *Village Voice* headline reads: "Why Gay Men Are Having Unsafe Sex Again." Eros, Thanatos. The drive for sex and love can entail a denial of death, which paradoxically may lead to death. I buy the paper and stare at a poster advertising a magazine called *Juggs*, filled with images of women with enormous breasts. The poster shows a busty woman and a man, John Wayne Bobbitt. Bobbitt is the man whose abused wife cut off his penis with a knife. He had his penis surgically reattached, and now he's starring in a porn movie called *John Wayne Bobbitt—Uncut.*

I don't want to think about the end of love at the beginning. But love and rejection are symbiotic, twins. Everyone wants to be loved and fears rejection, which precipitates an awful fall from grace. Ecstasy evaporates, as if it were never there. The telephone doesn't ring, it's over. I read once that Alain Delon sent Romy Schneider a single rose. Everyone knows about the end, it's always the same.

I don't want to relive, even as fantasy, the anguish, the sense of loss and violation in my body, the phantom physical pain, as if I actually had lost a piece of myself. I don't want to hear the monotonous dialogues and monologues playing in my mind. I can't stand the end. I hate love. Human beings are condemned to endless repetitions and stupidities, not only in love. But in love these repetitions and stupidities are grotesque, because the revelatory drop is fast, astoundingly deep, and hideous. We fall on our faces from a great height. We become distorted, disfigured. We don't recognize ourselves. The irony is that at first we didn't want to recognize ourselves, we wanted to lose ourselves, to be different people. I'd refuse romance, if it weren't so charming and seductive.

I walk home, recalling some of the men I've rejected. Sometimes I was insensitive. Sometimes I was horrible, but I was unable to stop myself. I must have been disappointed. The one who rejects is disheartened, too, furious at having lost again. I listen to the messages on my answering machine. Nothing exciting.

I want excitement. But I can't naively enter into this fantasy, concocted from ancient texts and fairy tales, from stories of hope and hopelessness, of longing fulfilled and longing eternally frustrated. I can't enter without suspicion. But I still want to make love the way people do in movies. And in dreams I know I'll be visited by an immortal beloved who would die for me or die without me. It's consoling that pain is more easily forgotten than pleasure, that the memory of pleasure lasts longer and with lustrous detail and vividness. There has to be some compensation for the terrible invention of love. I turn on the TV.

1995

16. That's How Strong His Love Is

The resistance to reading fiction may be a refusal to enter into another world, a strange place, where one must suspend one's own world, where one's world may be ignored. A novel speaks: This is a world not of your making. At the heartless center of fiction is a paradox, which is the writer's belief, a kind of reasoning, that since the "real world" is, in most ways, not of one's choosing, a fictive world is no less "real." Given this somewhat cynical, somewhat fabulous logic, a novel or a story is as credible, valid, or true as nonfiction—writing based on what actually occurs in life. Fiction's "truth" is verisimilitude, an appearance of truth, of likelihood.

In *Ready to Catch Him Should He Fall*, Englishman Neil Bartlett's first novel, truth rides a wild pony; it won't likely be fenced in. Characters don't reveal themselves; some events in the novel may or may not have happened, and motives are as various as emotions. The short of this novel, which contains many stories and ideas, is: *Ready* is a love story between two beautiful men, Boy and O (Older), set in a city like London, where gay men are under threat. Boy and O persevere, against all odds, to commit themselves to each other. They even marry. But can they and do they live happily ever after?

The reader has to say, "I want to see these two men together, I want that." And I go, "Right, that's all you've got. Whatever will come will come from that. Any politics will proceed from that . . ." I want people to be caught going, "I don't know why I'm crying. I'm crying because I want it to be true but I know it isn't true. Or I'm crying because I know it isn't true but suddenly I believe it could be true." Where you're caught in the conundrum of believing and not believing, and it just makes you laugh. Where you go . . . "That's completely ludicrous," then you go, "Wait, look, I've done that."

Much of the novel's action takes place in The Bar. It is a safe house to the men who are its habitués (a gay "Cheers"); a theater where dialogue and action can be staged (all the world's a stage, everyone's a player), and a make-believe home for Boy, Mother, and O. There's Father, too, but he mostly exists offstage, never frequenting The Bar. Instead, Father sends letters to Boy. These letters, like monologues in a play, or asides hissed in dark alleys, interrupt the narrative with another narrative—the story of a father and son. But is Father really Boy's father?

The family Bartlett creates—his tragic heroes, his soap opera stars—mimes and mocks, worships and parodies the conventional family. They stand in for but do not fill the places of fathers, mothers, and sons (there is no Girl or daughter). Excessive, they overflow those familiar spaces. Bartlett's characters are closer to allegorical figures; so big, bigger than life, they can't and don't need to be explained. They go beyond the scope of any mere novel.

From the beginning, Bartlett's impetuous narrator (neither O nor Boy) enjoins the reader to enter the novel, by asking "you" to look at a photograph of "this Boy of ours." Like the reader, the narrator is a spectator at The Bar, where Boy is introduced to and educated about his sexuality and the gay life, its pleasures, its vicissitudes. The narrator, an anonymous but not impartial voice, knows about "your" need for truth, for the real story. "You want to know that someone isn't just making the whole thing up when they talk about a man being that special to them."

The most obvious of *Ready*'s narrative plans is for "you" to be in the story too. You are asked to fit into its textual, extended family. *Ready* understands that you must want something when you read a book, or walk down a street, go to the theater or listen to music. It winds itself about your putative hungers as much as it articulates Bartlett's. It says: You are creatures of desire, constructed by your desires. Try these on for size.

My version of fiction is of readers being invited and seduced into constructing their own truth, and my version is relentlessly and unwarrantedly optimistic. I've been attacked [in England]— *Ready is too optimistic, too fantastic. It supposes that victory is possible. "Come off it. We should be writing books about the realistic, the nitty-gritty struggle of achieving political change."*

The narrator tells Boy's story, watches Boy couple with this man or that. He also watches Mother, who owns The Bar, as she guides Boy, keeping him under her ample, high-camp wing. Mother lends Boy books that both pose and answer implicit questions: how is one to be a gay man? who are one's influences? where are we in history? Boy is perplexed by the books, much as "you" might be by him or Mother.

Mother is a fascinating character whose partial life story, of resonant details, is woven into *Ready*. For instance, Mother always wears the same dress (she has five copies): "These dresses were the rest of [Mother's] life; she did not ever intend to change her dress, so to speak." Each night Mother's calculated appearance at The Bar is dramatic, an event worthy of a diva. (Which might make a reader, one like me, hypothesize: a mother is an event, always an occasion to the young child who needs her). In a proprietary— motherly—fashion, Mother inserts herself into the heart of the novel, Boy and O's relationship. They have of course met at The Bar. But why Mother takes a vital interest in the progress of their love affair, why she later pays their rent, why she lends them dresses one evening when they are to announce their love to The Bar (their true world), is ambiguous. She simply does what she does—acts the part of a mother—with these men who are not her "real" sons.

The narrator has the formidable job of recounting Boy and O's astounding, elaborate romance: "They had such a formal courtship." They dress painstakingly for each other. They think incessantly of each other. They make love in as many ways as they can imagine. They spend days and nights together, disappearing from The Bar. They attend shows, and Boy notices that "O avoided the family comedies and preferred tragedies, operas and farces, any genre in which the male characters are reduced or elevated to tears. Boy himself wanted shows full of loud music, expensive lighting, punishing dance routines executed by desperate and expert boys and girls, astonishing stages which rose and fell to reveal deep black spaces (Boy thought, *that's how my heart works*)."

Ready refers as much to plays and opera as it does to other books (especially those that have yet to be written). Drama, song, and performance saturate its pages: Boy and O describe what they see at the theater; Mother sings in The Bar, Father's letters stop the action the way monologues do. The novel is virtually part of Bartlett's ongoing performance in the world, his extensive literary project.

I think of all of my work as being of a piece. There is a moment in Ready, *on the night before they fall into each other's arms. O goes home through the subway station and sees the man who is collapsed on the floor. He's collapsed on the floor in a way that reminds him of a queen in a tragedy, and when I wrote that O says the line, "Oh intolerable"—I didn't know where that was from. After I wrote that I went on to be involved in producing Racine's* Berenice *at the National Theater, so it all comes home to roost. . . . And, in* Ready, *the woman in the theater who walks into a spotlight and sings her heart out, she appears in* Sarrasine. (Bartlett's play *Sarrasine* was based on Balzac's story.)

Bartlett's active engagement with drama started in college, at Oxford. The first play he wrote and put on, *Oscar's Seance*, was staged in Oscar Wilde's own rooms. Not long after, Bartlett made Wilde the subject of his first book, *Who Was That Man: A Present for Oscar Wilde*, which is technically not a fiction, but a history of or critical meditation on Oscar Wilde.

In *Who Was That Man*, Bartlett's wish to "find" the gay Wilde —
"he is famous above all else for being a homosexual" — is juxtaposed
with his need to find himself. His research — his "cruising" — of
Wilde takes place in the library, "the place I started looking for
my story." An occasion for Bartlett's own story of contemporary
gay life, Wilde is a historical figure through whom Bartlett can
"see" himself, and other men, darkly. "Although his London is a
very different place . . . his life there, like ours, is written in code."
In a sense Wilde himself is mere evidence, but significant evidence
for Bartlett that men like him and his friends exist, have existed,
and more, that they can and do love each other. "If we don't learn
anything from history then it is because we don't know any history."

Ready does not take up where the Wilde book leaves off, but,
as Virginia Woolf assured us books do, continues it. In *Who Was
That Man*, Bartlett asks, "But what if the Soho queen had talked
of love? Imagine whispering to another man: I want you to take
care of me." Boy and O whisper to each other of their need to be
taken care of. The novel revels in writing down what should not
be spoken between men. It wants to take heart and give in to
heart, to emphasize, as Boy puts it, "That's how the heart works."

A metaphor for pleasure, heart battles "reality." When Boy and
O go to the theater, they wait for that "very special moment, in
which a woman would be caught in a spotlight, and would sing,
well, would just sing her heart out . . . they knew that it was for
them, somehow, that she sang: for their condition." But on any of
those evenings, when they are at The Bar or in a theater, a gay
man might be attacked in the city: "This time there was no knife,
they just got him on the floor and it was just a fist which had come
down on the man's face again and again."

Still, the greatest threat to their union — and their "condition" —
may be Father. Father is the novel's mystery man, an avenging and
sympathetic angel, a disembodied presence composed of words.
An epistolary novel all by itself, his letters to "this Boy of ours"
(or this Boy of O's) rip into their love story. When finally Boy
forces him to live with them, Father's "actual" presence savages
their relationship as a wild beast might its prey. Why does Boy

bring him to their home? Because Father is enfeebled? Because Boy wants to help him die? Because he wants to kill him, as one must kill one's symbolic father? Father's truth is cruel and elusive; he's the most difficult figure in the book.

Quelle surprise that it should be Father. I don't want to justify or explain what I'm doing with that character. Every gay man I know has a relationship of unspeakable complexity [with his father]—*every man I know—and a huge component is rage. Father's the most fantastic of all the characters. He must die before they can live together. He must die in their arms. If he dies beyond their ken, if he simply absented himself, then that would not solve the problem. In my experience that's a very deep thing with a lot of gay men. It's not that your father must get out of your life and be in another city, and "Fuck him, he no longer has any control over me." He has to die in your arms. Now in my case my father has died in my arms, that is, that patriarchal father who forbade me to be who I am has died. But my own father is still alive and has appeared with me on TV as my father in a fictional piece called* That's How Strong My Love Is. *One of the scenes was me sitting with my father on a sofa, saying, "When I was a little boy you wanted me to grow up to be like you and now I haven't and I love you," and I take hold of my father's hand and there's a closeup of my father's face with tears in his eyes. His face dissolves into my face and of course I look exactly like him, we have the same face. I will look exactly like my father when I'm his age.*

Toward the end of *Ready*, some time after Father's death, Boy and O walk through the city. On this night, "inexplicably no one stared at them when they paused to kiss under the strings of colored lights by the river. And when they got home at 4 a.m. the night did not end for them . . . they were for that night and for several other nights of that remarkable year perfect, perfect, perfect." This night of perfection and their marriage, a perfect union, are the probable sources for the charge of "optimism" against the novel that Bartlett mentioned.

I will get two letters in one week. One says, "I want to tell you that I have been with the same man for 35 years now, and when I read the closing passage of your book I want to tell you that you have described our love together." And I get another letter, which says, "I cannot read the end of your book, I am so hurt, I am so angry. We can't even walk down the street together. Last week I was attacked again. I can't stand it any longer."

Ready is by definition political; "polis" means life in the city. But Bartlett's is an imaginary city, a phantasm, reminiscent in its wildly dark and ecstatic representational excesses of films by fellow gay Englishman Derek Jarman, particularly *Sebastiane, The Last of England*, and *The Garden*. Lyrical and tough as Jarman's work is, *Ready*, in its urgency, is like a letter to England, a manifesto disguised as a narrative, filled with love and hate, a *cri de coeur*. For me, not being, among other things, English, male, or gay, it is not optimistic. Though hope may spring eternal, it is fragile; the unwieldy longing for love and safety in an inhospitable and violent world seems likely to go unfulfilled. Boy and O's long walk through the city ends a contemporary fable, a fairy tale, one Oscar Wilde might have written. Sadness emanates from its exquisite quest for perfection, for beauty.

For this one night they went out and instead of the world being the city where you're walking down the street, after just having made love, and someone says to you "Queer"—and that's it, it's all taken away from you. In Ready *the reverse happens, the city is turned into a carnival, and for once the city seems to be operating on their laws.*

The beautiful, exacting, passionate relationship between Boy and O—magical and mythical—exists within the bounds of the city, within limits, in a world not of their making. Bartlett sets his fiction among other fictions—other art and books—and within the so-called real world. Criticism of his work as "fantastic" strikes at the paradox of fiction and at verisimilitude. For his fiction requires, I think, that one try to imagine something different from what actually exists. His "truths"—his pleasures—argue with "reality." *Ready* relies on Bartlett's fictive willing, and on fantasy, "daytime phantasies" which, like dreams, as Freud put it, "are wish-fulfillments" and "benefit by a certain degree of relaxation of censorship." In his version of the fantastic, Bartlett envisions beauty, which in these times is hard to imagine and often seems irrelevant.

My primary concern is to create beauty. I want people who read my book to be aroused sexually; I want them to cry. And then they can read under, over, and around it every kind of constructed relation to their own lives.

It is as if Bartlett relentlessly asks: If we have a role to play in our own lives, shouldn't we imagine beauty too? Does beauty have a place in our futures? Thinking about his work and about beauty, I was reminded of a recent essay by filmmaker and theorist Trinh T. Minh-ha, which ends: "By indulging in beauty, limiting its access and ownership to connoisseurship, by taking it for granted, or by rejecting it as a form of luxury, declaring thereby that its power is irrevocably dead (since it has served too long as an escapist tool to protect the breed of experts called 'esthetes'), one so impoverishes oneself as to be deprived even of that which cannot be possessed and remains formless form. This . . . must then be named, in the context of material abundance and overdevelopment, the Other Poverty." Bartlett's writing addresses that poverty.

1991

All italicized quotes are Neil Bartlett's from an interview with Lynne Tillman.

17. Call It Local/ *Specter of the Rose*

Being a many-sided writer has drawbacks. You achieve no
easily admired mannerism. Critics cannot write illuminatingly
of your "style." And "inconsistency" makes you seem to many
no artist at all. An artist, it is believed, must have an unvarying
embrace of life.

> —Ben Hecht, from his preface to
> *A Treasury of Ben Hecht*

The film *Specter of the Rose* seems to have been hatched from
two short stories by Hecht: "Specter of the Rose" and "Some Slightly
Crazy People." The first is a tragic tale of madness and murder, a
drama about a ballet dancer called Sanine, who is compared with
Nijinsky. The second, "Some Slightly Crazy People," presents the
hilarious ordeals of Max Poliakoff, unsuccessful theater producer,
and his sidekick/love, La Sylph, a ballet mistress, as they try to
produce a play by a reluctant-to-be-performed playwright. The
film is a hybrid, or, to use a different metaphor, it's a merger. And
as in mergers, when two companies selling different products come
together as one, there are unintended consequences. A merger of

Hecht's many-sidedness, *Specter of the Rose* is full of such unintended consequences. Inconsistent and with an embrace of life that makes reckless turns from comedy to tragedy and suspense and back, it's funny when it should be serious.

Even the hero's name is a joke, for while it is a real Russian name, Sanine is also an anagram for insane. Sanine is crazy, mad as a loon, and he wants to kill his new bride, Heidi, whenever he hears his favorite ballet music "Specter of the Rose." The cops are on to him, but he has his defenders, Poliakoff (played by Michael Chekhov) among them, who, when he learns from the police that Sanine has been saying he murdered his first wife, proclaims: "Every great artist goes through a period like this, when he doesn't make sense. What do you expect?" Lionel, the poet (played by Lionel Stander), who's brought the police to the ballet studio to find Sanine, answers: "The lunacy of great artists usually produces masterpieces, not murders." It's a great line, of course—the film is full of them— and it establishes Lionel as a hardboiled foil to the romantics Poliakoff and La Sylph, who also defends Sanine.

There's a show-must-go-on mentality infusing this film. Even though Sanine is almost certainly a murderer, he's an artist, a great artist, who must be allowed to perform. Which makes Poliakoff's question, "What do you expect [from artists]?" a more general one that we, in the audience, might consider while watching this film. Lionel may believe in masterpieces, but he's not one to place artists above the law.

On the other hand, he does support poetry over politics, and figures in another one of the film's arguments or subtexts. After the wedding party for Sanine and Heidi, with whom Lionel is in love, Lionel and the set designer Kropotkin drunkenly debate poetry, politics, and the masses:

Kropotkin: You're only one man suffering. When the masses suffer, then the suffering counts.

Lionel: The suffering of the masses is a minor phenomenon beside one man's tears. . . .

Kropotkin: The masses would never get married if the poets didn't tell them how beautiful it was.

Lionel complains that "people think of the governments of China and Russia, instead of themselves. . . . This amateur confusion is called social consciousness." While Hecht is satirizing political arguments that were rife in Hollywood and New York in the theater and film worlds in the thirties and forties, the very fact that this dialogue exists in this film is important, particularly for historical reasons.

Specter of the Rose was released in 1946, a year after the war ended, the year Nixon defeated Helen Gahagan Douglas through red-baiting, and a year before the Hollywood Ten were forced to go to Washington to testify before Congress. With McCarthy still on the horizon, the film's playfulness about politics and the masses may mark the end of an era—at least its representation in Hollywood films. I doubt that there was any film made after 1946/ 47 with this kind of insouciance about ideas that might, very shortly, mark someone as a Red. For once red-baiting was in full swing, certain ideas (as well, of course, as writers and actors and directors) would disappear from the Hollywood screen.

Another piece of history that figures in this film: the Russians had been our allies during WWII. They were also dominant in ballet. In *Specter of the Rose* half the characters have Russian names, even when they're Americans of non-Russian descent— Sanine is really Paul Dixon from Indiana—which demonstrates not only Americans wanting to emulate Russian dancers, but also a friendliness between the two nations. Again it's 1946, not 1948, or 1949, and so on into the Cold War, and it's still feasible, permissible, to represent the Russians as good guys.

While U.S. and world politics enter this picture through the back door, so to speak, sexual politics enters through the front door. After all Sanine wants to kill women, not men. Or, specifically, wants to kill wives. (I can't help but imagine Ben Hecht's going through a bad divorce, and all those G.I.'s coming back from the war, finding their wives in jobs that once were theirs.) There's a lot of talk about wives, love, and marriage, and Poliakoff, again defending Sanine, says: "What husband have you known who hasn't wanted to kill his wife? That is definitely part of marriage." Johnny

Carson might use a line like that in one of his monologues. But it's no joke that some men do kill their wives, and maybe more fantasize it. Madness is associated with art and creativity, and men want to kill women. These ideas are so imbricated in our lives and culture, they're not particularly surprising or shocking. They're like wallpaper. But to Ben Hecht's credit, if Sanine did murder his first wife, we don't see it. What we do see is Sanine *not murdering* his second wife, Heidi. She's fallen asleep on the bed in a second-rate hotel room, and he's having a psychotic episode. He hears the tune in his head, dances a little, places the knife at Heidi's neck, struggles with himself, leaps away, then dances around the room and up the walls and out the window, rather than slashing Heidi to death. He has beaten down his evil half, the half of him he claims is bad but not-him, and has become a male suicide, a rarity in film compared with the murdered female. The film-noir lighting and camera angles at times create a sense of danger for Heidi—in one shot she literally stands in Sanine's shadow—but one rarely feels frightened for her. Even when La Sylph tries to warn her about Sanine (after, not before, the marriage), it's comical:

La Sylph: There's something much more important in your life now than love. Your husband is a madman.

Heidi: I wish you hadn't said that.

Though La Sylph is acted by Judith Anderson, even she can't make the line, "Your husband is a madman," ominous; I laugh each time I watch the scene. And it doesn't help that Heidi's response sounds as if it's coming from another movie, one directed by Emily Post, famous for her books on etiquette.

It's forty years after *Specter of the Rose* was made, and it strikes me that one could say it's dated. But why does something look and sound dated? It's not only to do with the changing politics of representation, although that's part of it. I can sense Ben Hecht's ambivalent presence in this film; he's asking questions that bother him. What's art? Am I an artist, here in Hollywood? Do I care about the masses? And so on. But rather than call this film "personal," which would place it in an already-defined category of film I don't think this is, I'll call it "local." It's located in Hecht's backyard, addressing a community rather than a world market. Along with an address, it has a specific time and place, and exists within a particular historical moment. So it is, almost literally, dated, and in a way, fascinating to watch because of that.

1987

18. Thoroughly Modern Meals: *The Futurist Cookbook*

Thinking about F.T. Marinetti, I'm reminded of an incident in London. Some years ago I saw a play there based on Kafka's diaries. The theater was on the eighth floor of an office building. The elevator operator, noting the floor I wanted, complained, "Everybody talks about Kafka but no one does anything about him." What does one do about Marinetti? An anarchist, a poet, an innovator, a fascist, an antifeminist, a superpatriot, a drum major for war, a "master" of the manifesto, as he was called, the progenitor of the Futurists is no easy figure to gloss.

With the first Futurist manifesto, published in 1909 on the front page of *Le Figaro*, Marinetti gave voice to a movement that celebrated the machine, that ecstatically embraced technology and war, a movement that saw itself as the New incarnate. The sculptor Boccioni was "nauseated by old walls and palaces, old motives, reminiscences." Marinetti chose the automobile over Samothrace.

The Futurist Cookbook by F.T. Marinetti. Translated by Suzanne Brill. Edited by Lesley Chamberlain. San Francisco: Bedford Arts, 1989.

Equipped with some 19th-century baggage—including an uncritical belief in progress—the Futurists emerged at the doorstep of a new century, ours.

Futurism may be carrying undue weight now, given its position at the start of the 20th century, when modernity was burdened with trying to become modern. To "make it new," as Ezra Pound exhorted. In the '30s movie *The Twentieth Century*—which takes place on a train of the same name—the conductor keeps repeating, when there's any problem, "But we're on the 20th Century," and passengers insist, "But this is the 20th Century." The movie asks: What makes us modern (or for that matter, postmodern)?

With *The Futurist Cookbook*, published first in 1932 and just now translated into English, Marinetti and others propose recipes for modernity, manifestos for the table. Through stories and recipes, they polemicize against traditions of all sorts, particularly those of the bourgeoisie, and offer Futurist maps to the entrance of the new. There's a recipe for "Words-In-Liberty," by the Futurist Aeropoet Escadame, which calls for "three sea dates, a half-moon of red watermelon, a thicket of radicchio, a little cube of Parmesan, a little sphere of gorgonzola, 8 tiny balls of caviare, 2 figs, 5 amaretti di Saronno biscuits: all arranged neatly on a large bed of mozzarella, to be eaten, eyes closed, letting one's hands wander here and there, while the great painter and word-in-liberty poet Depero recites his famous song 'Jacopson.' " There's "Steel Chicken"—the flavor of steel is an important ingredient in any machine lover's diet— "mechanized by aluminum-colored bonbons." And my favorite, by Marinetti, "RAW MEAT TORN BY TRUMPET BLASTS":

> (C)ut a perfect cube of beef. Pass an electric current through it, then marinate it for twenty-four hours in a mixture of rum, cognac, and white vermouth. Remove it from the mixture and serve on a bed of red pepper, black pepper and snow. Each mouthful is to be chewed carefully for one minute and each mouthful is divided from the next by vehement blasts on the trumpet blown by the eater himself.... The soldiers are served plates of ripe persimmons, pomegranates, and blood oranges. While these disappear into their mouths, some very

sweet perfumes . . . will be sprayed around the room, the nostalgic and decadent sweetness of which will be roughly rejected by the soldiers who rush like lightning to put their gas masks on.

Trumpet blasts, soldiers and ripe persimmons, gas masks and perfumes of nostalgia characterize the Futurist menu of the 1930s: a tempting mix of militarism, sensuality, art, and nature. The cookbook aims for a "culinary revolution . . . changing radically the eating habits of our race." Speed, motion, light, and liberty are constant companions, part of any dinner. Futurist cooking is "tuned to high speeds like the motor of a hydroplane." Marinetti promises eating that is art, "the art of self-nourishment," which, "like all the arts . . . eschews plagiarism and demands creative originality." These are important ingredients in the recipe for Modernism—the "art of self-nourishment" is by any other name reflexivity.

"Since everything in modern civilization tends toward the elimination of weight and increased speed, the cooking of the future must conform to the ends of evolution." Pasta is banned. Pastasciutta is "a passéist food because it makes people heavy, brutish . . . skeptical, slow, pessimistic." The Futurists are for risotto, or "totalrice." Rice is light, good for speed and action, and, it's noted, there's an Italian rice industry to consider as well.

Marinetti deploys food to construct "the modern man," the new subject, to build him from the inside out, where food is metaphor and fuel. Futurist Marco Rampereti asserts: "The allegorical Italian has always got his avid mouth wide open over a plate of tagliatelle when he isn't dangling dripping strands of vermicelli down his greedy gullet. . . . Our pasta is like our rhetoric, only good for filling up our mouths." Since Marinetti is the poet who advanced the idea of "parole in liberta," it makes sense that food might be seen as rhetoric. Using certain words and dropping others, like dropping pasta and adding rice, might signify departures and surprises, changes in thinking, changes in being.

In the new diet, what's on the menu isn't only food. Like art, food must strive to interact with its environment, and the environment itself must be designed to serve higher ends—

Marinetti's evolution of society. At a Futurist dinner all the senses must be engaged and taught to renounce the habits that dull pleasure. One might sit bathed in "an unexpected green light" while an airplane motor roars the song of machines. Under a Futurist regime, where knives and forks are passé, guests could be asked to touch the leg of the guest next to them or, when having "Fillia's Aerofood . . . composed of different fruits and vegetables," to eat "with the right hand . . . while the left hand caresses a tactile surface made of sandpaper, velvet and silk. Meanwhile the orchestra plays a noisy, wild jazz . . ."

The Holy Palate Restaurant, sometimes known as the Aluminum Restaurant, site of actual Futurist dinners, served "sculpted meat," which is "symbolic of Italian regions." Although these antic dinners and wild proclamations are meant to be taken with a dollop of the zany, where there's style there's content, and Marinetti isn't content with jokes. He demands: "The word Italy must rule over the word Liberty! . . . a) The word Italy must rule over the word genius. b) The word Italy must rule over the word intelligence. c) The word Italy must rule over the words culture and statistics. d) The word Italy must rule over the word truth."

It's an odd position from the man who called for words in liberty, words freed from syntax. But not an odd position for a fascist. His "words in liberty" become fixed in a new syntax, that of the State. Marinetti was, after all, one of the first members of the Fascist party, and his own words, instead of being freed from history, resonate with it. They taste, for instance, of the bitter aftermath of the Great War and Italy's sense of betrayal by the Allies. In 1932, this past also included the deaths of leading Futurists Boccioni and Sant'Elia, both of whom, like so many others, had enthusiastically rushed to battle. The Great War effectively put an end to the most productive moment of Futurism, so it's not surprising that Marinetti calls for the murder of nostalgia. The Futurist door to modernity, once pried open and walked through, must be shut forever on the past—past failures and past losses.

As Marinetti wrote, "It is not by chance this work is published during a world economic crisis." His "antidote" to despair is "a

Futurist way of cooking, that is, optimism at the table." It's
significant that the book begins with a parable entitled "The Dinner
That Stopped a Suicide." Giulio is obsessed with killing himself,
as "She" has died in New York—at that time a place of many
capitalist suicides—and is "calling" to him to join her. So Marinetti,
Prampolini, and Fillia, the "Aeropainters", rush to their friend's
home. At the same time, another "She," one "who resembles" the
first, sends Giulio a message of hope. But Giulio says he must "kill
himself tonight." "Unless?" the Aeropainters ask. And Marinetti
turns to Giulio, "Unless you take us instantly to your splendid,
well-stocked kitchens." A hilarious retort to a singular cul-de-sac
and a worldwide depression, or a comic way out of the numbing
effects of the past.

It's not without consequence, either, that death in the suicide
story is represented by She. Women are always other in Futurism,
(though sometimes [m]other): they sit uneasily at its table,
occasionally having to eat food shaped like their own bodies. The
first Futurist Manifesto proclaimed: "We will glorify war—the
world's only hygiene—militarism, patriotism, the destructive genius
of freedom-bringers, beautiful ideas worth dying for, and scorn
for women.... We will destroy... feminism." And it's not just
coincidence that the call against death also comes from a She,
"one who resembles her." This may be a reference to capitalism
under a fascist state. But in any case, the female body signifies
danger and death as well as renewal. In the "Geographic Dinner,"
She's a waitress, "a shapely young woman dressed in a long white
tunic on which a complete geographical map of Africa has been
drawn in color, it enfolds her entire body." This is a neat
conflation—woman as Africa, then a site of Italian colonies. That
part of the world is turned into something to be devoured, the
waitress colony providing food to be greedily eaten up like a woman
might be by a hungry lover. Women, like food, are figures of speech.

The second-wave Futurists, like the first, disdained women. But
while the first-wave Futurists embraced both internationalism and
war, the second wave were "Italy Firsters." They call for an end to
Xenomania, defined in the cookbook as "the international cuisine

of grand hotels," which in Italy is submitted to "only because it comes from abroad." Xenomanes are anti-Italians, like Arturo Toscanini, who "disown(ed) his own national hymns . . . opportunistically playing foreign anthems"; those who don't "promote Italian influence in the world" and "who are infatuated with foreign customs and snobbisms." The second-wave Futurists trounce some traditions, including the earlier Futurists' internationalism, but they remain true to the belief in an overpowering principle that centers existence. For Marinetti, it's not a belief in God but in the State—specifically, Italy under Mussolini. As Hannah Arendt put it: "The Fascist movement, a 'party above parties' . . . identified itself with the highest national authority, and tried to make the whole people 'part of the state.' "

To make Italians into, and part of, a healthy state, Marinetti wants to put the nation on a diet that surpasses food. Like most diet books and cookbooks, *The Futurist Cookbook* is sometimes repetitive, hammering away at its prescriptions for right living with short announcements that read like ads. In this case, ads for the State. Eating ought to imbue patriotic feeling—as in, the way to the heart is through the stomach.

And speaking of the heart, the entire cookbook is a prescription for the regulation of pleasure. While everything in it seems to be full of imagination, fun, and cleverness, not that much is really left to the imagination. We're told not only what to eat but how to and with what feelings, in what kind of restaurant, listening to what type of music, and sniffing what kind of scents. The "New Year's Eve Dinner," for instance, is meant to overturn crusty bourgeois conventions, when "the same elements have conspired to produce a happiness which has been enjoyed too often." So, "everyone eats in compulsory silence: the desire for noise and jollity is suppressed." Humorously disguised as a call to the anarchic, the dinner program substitutes one kind of order for another. Marinetti, whose words are supposedly "in liberty," sets down a regimen—tongue in cheek—for the right libertinage. He optimistically ordains a future of aluminum and steel, of controlled pleasure and virility, of art that scoffs at tradition in search of the genuinely contemporary, all palatable to the State.

Here at the end of this century, some of these refrains may not seem unfamiliar. Though since we're at the end of it, that's supposed to mean something in itself, the way death means something: *We're at the end of the Twentieth Century!* Which reminds me again of that movie of the same name.

In the time after modernism, otherwise known as postmodernism, certain beliefs—especially faith in the new, in progress, in self-referentiality—have come under scrutiny and are back at the train station, with a bad wheel or engine. Some of the cars have become derailed or separated from each other. But can anything be left behind, and what's in front and what's in back? Does coming to the end of a century have anything to do with an end anyway? Will a postmodern menu offer us something different, other metaphors, like one from column A, column B, and column C? Do recipes with generous amounts of asymmetries and hardy dashes of anticlosure avoid being recipes?

This reading is compelled by forces from within and without; I see the past through my version of the present. A recipe may be inscribed in me that I'm unaware of and its powerful ingredients may simply, unconsciously, overwhelm me. For instance, I'm still playing with trains and recipes. And maybe I ought to be at the end of, at least, this trope.

1989

19. The Autobiography of Eve

A Mind of My Own is the autobiography of Chris Costner Sizemore, better known as "Eve." Sizemore was the case study upon which *The Three Faces of Eve*, a popular 1957 movie directed by Nunnally Johnston, was based. Joanne Woodward played Eve, winning an Academy Award for her virtuoso performance as a woman under the influence of a mental illness, Multiple Personality Disorder (MPD). In the movie Woodward metamorphosed, before the camera and without special effects, from Eve Black, "the party girl," to Eve White, "the mother/wife," to Jane, "the intellectual woman," enacting a female Jekyll, Jekyll, and Hyde as constituted through a psychiatric/cinematic lens.

Sizemore has been dogged by her cinematic representative "Eve," who made her a celebrity, although no one knew who she was—Sizemore didn't go public until the mid-'70s—and, more disturbing, neither did she. In a sense her life has been mediated, if not constructed, by the movie that gave her "fame in anonymity."[1] (Her books prior to this one are entitled *The Final Face of Eve* and *I'm Eve*.) Sizemore was supposed to have been cured of MPD by her first psychiatrists, Corbett H. Thigpen and Hervey M. Cleckley, which is what *The Three Faces of Eve* portrays; and Lee J. Cobb, playing the psychiatrist who discovers her illness and works through it with her, is nearly as much its star/hero as Eve. But *A Mind of My Own* tells another tale: Sizemore writes that it took twenty more years for her to overcome MPD, to become, as she puts it, "unified."

Ironically, Sizemore did not see the movie until November 16, 1974, an event of great meaning to her and her family, and one carefully documented in the book. "My alters" (her other personalities), she writes, "had been barred from its world premiere in Augusta, Georgia, because Drs. Thigpen and Cleckley believed that seeing it could be highly detrimental to the stability of the patient who, they had wrongly claimed, was cured."

Sizemore's book takes up her life after the movie and explains how she worked through her illness with her new analyst, Dr. Tony A. Tsitos, how she strove to bring together her alters, to allow her various personalities to find expression or representation through just one conduit or self. After unification, her newly won self learns the difficulty of existing in the so-called real world. She must make amends with her husband, who has, in a sense, been married to many wives — "whichever one was 'out' was my wife" — and to her children, both of whom, she explains, were given birth to by alters and had formed attachments to their alter-mothers and to others of her personalities. With a new psyche in place, Sizemore now pursues a career as a painter (some of her alters had painted), making work that represents her former illness and current "wellness." In addition to painting, Sizemore actively campaigns for the mentally ill, especially the sufferers of MPD, speaking in front of large audiences around the country as an advocate for their rights and their ability to be helped. She has also worked hard to get MPD recognized as a bona fide mental illness, to make the disorder exist in representation not just as a movie but in the

1. All quotations of Chris Costner Sizemore, or of her husband, are taken from Chris Costner Sizemore, *A Mind of My Own* (New York: William Morrow, 1989).

annals of the psychiatric establishment. (In 1980, MPD entered the medical language by way of the APA's handbook, the DSM, as 300.14 Multiple Personality.)

The issue of representation in all its complexity is critical to Sizemore's life, and its multiple meanings show themselves throughout her book, a book in which she speaks of her own multiplicity. MPD itself, understood as an intrapsychic battle waged over mind and body by warring selves or representations, is a condition that embodies such issues. As Sizemore recounts her life she often compares herself with the movie Eve, with whom she seems at times to have a kind of sibling rivalry. (Even after she is unified, she is given presents by her husband and family in the name of that alter.) She likens herself to celebrities—Liz Taylor, for one—in a conscious effort to emulate successful female role models. She presents herself as "cured patient," as "artist," as "writer," as "normal woman, wife and mother," to public, family, and friends. Overwhelming at times is Sizemore's need to achieve representation and to make representations in the world—in all of these guises. "In short, I struggled to be all things to all people." A Mind of My Own showcases a dizzying display of what she has done and who has praised her, making this reader wonder whether the self, once unified, is almost destined to become self-congratulatory.

Perhaps to offset this burgeoning narcissism, Sizemore's preferred mode of writing the self is the quote. Like literary devices, the many alters are in a sense already quotations. These personalities offer their thoughts through Sizemore, as memories and dialogue, or through their diaries and notes. When their voices enter, paragraphs read like sketches for bizarre sitcoms in which characters such as Retrace Lady, Strawberry Girl, or Purple Lady vie for "point of view" or dominance.

But even when not representing the alters, who are in a way the unconscious quotations, Sizemore writes her life as a series of quotes. Rather than saying what she thinks, she cites herself having said the thought at another time. Or instead of incorporating into her narrative someone else's comments about her, she puts their sometimes innocuous remarks in quotes. The curved marks of punctuation distance the reader from her words and set off the ideas as if they had arrived from far away. The effect is to make the unified self Sizemore so urgently wants recognition for a fabrication of fragments and statements, an aggregate of impressions rather than a seamless unity. It may not be the result she desired, but it is a better reflection of the problems of the constructed self and of representing that self. Overall, the use of quotation attests to her desire for authenticity. In this regard the book's ultimate sentence is striking—again in someone else's words: "Chris Sizemore is real."

Having engaged successfully with the psychiatric institution, Sizemore may be ready for her current entanglement—with the law. Some years ago Sissy Spacek, the actress, expressed a desire to make a film of Sizemore's life since *The Three Faces of Eve*. But Twentieth-Century Fox has refused to allow the project to go forward, insisting that the studio owns the rights to Sizemore's life story, which Sizemore, at the time the movie was made, signed over to them. To add to the obvious irony of a fight to own her life story—"claiming my own history"—is the injury that might have been done to her by the psychiatrists who negotiated the contract for her, when they stood to gain as much if not more from it than she.

Sizemore's legal argument is that one of her alters, Jane, signed the contract, and that she was not yet cured of her illness. When it comes to trial, the case will most likely rest upon the issue of her competence at that time. But in *A Mind of My Own* Sizemore may have logically contradicted her own defense. Asked by the FBI, in February 1982, to evaluate the case of Kenneth Bianchi—the serial murderer known as the Hillside Strangler, who claimed to have MPD—she recounts her position (she thought he was a fake) and also her feelings about the "not guilty by reason of insanity" plea. As to whether a person with MPD "could have determined right from wrong" and "be held responsible for those acts," Sizemore answers, "Unlike schizophrenics, MPD patients do not lose touch with reality, and most of their alters can tell right from wrong. So, yes, I believe he should have been held responsible for his acts." Should Sizemore now be held responsible for the act of a competent alter? Or was that alter incompetent? What's true?

If Chris Sizemore's story reads as much like fiction as "real life," it may be because truth or reality isn't opposed to fiction. Sizemore's "cases" pose truth itself as a complex of representations whose interpretations will always be informed by the institutions that define reality. And Reality and its fraternal twin, Representation, undergo continuous overhaul. Sizemore's struggles within different discourses are played out on a broad field where the battle over, and the critique of, representation is waged. That current field includes movies such as *Everybody Wins*, in which Debra Winger's character flips from one personality to another — raunchy prostitute, wholesome do-gooder, pedantic sadist. Her romantic partner, Nick Nolte, doesn't know what's hit him, along with the audience, which is elliptically clued in, an hour into the film, that Winger's character is more than just whimsical. But her "craziness" is never referred to as MPD or indeed named anything at all. The representation of an unnamed disorder fuses with familiar fantasies and fears of women, conjuring psychoanalyst Joan Riviere's "femininity as masquerade" as the horror-movie theme of the '90s. Sizemore might be horrified by this casual usage of MPD, where personality changes become just so many plot points.

"Everybody wins" certainly won't be the outcome of her court case, as it probably won't be the conclusion to the struggle for representation itself.

1990

20. | The Real McCoy

From the universe of possible reasons for a book's going out of print, there might be collected an anthology in cultural politics, with a chapter for "unpopular culture." One could imagine Horace McCoy there, as all his work is OP, even his famous-for-a-minute Depression-era marathon dance novel, *They Shoot Horses, Don't They?* (1935), which returned to print, briefly, with the movie of the same name. Collectors know a real find: McCoy's *I Should Have Stayed Home*, sitting in a used bookstore on a dusty shelf, positioned somewhere between Precious and Obscure Oblivion. My paperback copy's cover proclaims it "Hard boiled," "Perverse," "Shockingly Brutal."

The hardboiled McCoy, if he was—we can't know the real McCoy—might have appreciated his oblivion. Cynicism and despair suffuse his novels, and a sad literary fate might have satisfied his pessimism. In its darkness the hardboiled school previewed film noir, in its cool toughness it rehearsed the next war and constructed future Cold Warriors. McCoy's writing is also self-conscious and reflexive—modernist—showing the influences of Hemingway and even Stein. His lean, taut style serves the genre, but what's interesting about his novels is their mix of literary forms. His work is not easy to categorize.

I Should Have Stayed Home appeared in 1938. Hitler was threatening Europe, and the U.S. was slowly moving out of the Depression, from isolationism toward war. This is the novel's time; its location, Hollywood—the Hollywood of extras. McCoy's truly marginal characters are drawn there by the movie world's promise of fame and fortune, not unlike Steinbeck's Okies in *Of Mice and Men*, who also went West hoping for salvation.

Ambitious antihero Ralph Carston wants it all, but his conscience and idealism stand in the way. Roommate Mona is much more stalwart. The novel begins with her and their mutual friend, Dorothy, going to jail; Dorothy for shoplifting, Mona for objecting loudly, in court, to Dorothy's sentence. Mona's disappearance into jail sets Ralph adrift, and he descends into the abyss: "Feeling the way I did, alone and friendless, with the future very black, I didn't want to get out on the streets and see what the sun had to show me, a cheap town filled with cheap stores and cheap people, like the town I had left, identically like any one of ten thousand other small towns in the country—not my Hollywood, not the Hollywood you read about."

Temptation enters Ralph the extra's life in the guise of an older woman. Mrs. Smithers is "filthy" rich with all the best movie connections. Embellishing this filthiness is how she takes her pleasure—she loves getting slapped around by gigolos. McCoy uses the novel's filmic context by having Mrs. Smithers seduce Ralph with pornographic home movies. Ralph succumbs, not quickly, not completely, and not, finally, successfully—he doesn't get a part but he also doesn't ever give up. And throughout the novel, Mona, as chorus or superego, warns him against Mrs. Smithers and himself; the two extras' dialogues construct a kind of argument about how far and how much are okay in the pursuit of success.

Relatively plotless, though replete with the genre's dark mayhem—suicide, court scenes, jail for Ralph—the story is primarily a journey, Ralph's making his way, or not making it, in the world. In this *Pilgrim's Progress*, the hero's struggle is not with God and the devil but with the secular world. McCoy uses Hollywood as the paradigm, the apotheosis, of capitalist society at a time when the myth of Horatio Alger was becoming a maudlin and corroded irony.

Ralph's battle with his own corruption and loss of principle is key to McCoy's work generally. His protagonists fight the good fight. In *I Should Have Stayed Home,* Mona refuses to be interviewed by fan magazines and rails against them for creating false and insatiable longings. A friend of Mona's, Johnny Hill, who does publicity for a studio, quits his job because a German consul was able to have censored a part of a movie in which "German youngsters [are] drilled as soldiers."

Then, in the reflexive mode, Johnny announces to Mona and Ralph that he's going to write a novel about Hollywood's extras— "the true story of this town concerns people like you—a girl like you and a boy like him. Maybe I'll put you two in a book. . . . Understand I don't think I've got any special talent for novel-writing." Ralph-in-Hollywood is McCoy's meditation on desire and failure. Though failure may now be the unspeakable of our society, in the midst of the Depression it was an existential fact of life. McCoy's Hollywood is the nightmare machine that produces phonies, monsters and wasted youth, sadness and sadism. He sees failure embedded within the system; there will always be people who don't make it.

McCoy's version of cultural politics is, like the country he's from, contradictory. There's some "conventional" racism, homo-phobia, and misogyny side by side with sympathy for the underdog and hope for a nationwide new deal. Contemporary "conventional" attitudes are as questionable but more difficult to isolate from the narratives—ideologies—that we live. It seems easier to spot offensive or questionable ideas in work from earlier periods, in part because language and style change. Concepts such as "underdog" and "phoney" may seem dated in today's parlance and in our nation, as presidents wrap themselves in symbols and commit highly unsymbolic Housing and Urban Development and savings and loan frauds. And get away with it. It's banal now even to say that corruption is endemic when many are positioned as permanent underdogs, the underclass.

Reading McCoy returns one to the not-so-distant past and to another consciousness. McCoy's sometimes uncomfortable speeches, prejudices, and "old-fashioned" language bespeak the U.S.'s disturbed history, its citizens' noble and ignoble values. His writing style itself speaks a very American language, presaging the Beats; long flowing sentences and moody lyricism alternate with terse, plain speech. Like other American writers from the transcendentalists on, McCoy eulogizes a disappearing America, its hometowns and daily life transformed by powerful economic and social forces. Hardboiled despair is personal, political, and unpopular. But given our economy, McCoy's lessons on living with failure might come in handy.

1990

21. Telling Tales

There's a series of Dewars ads on telephone booths around NY. One shows a guy with a lampshade on his head. It says: Remember that party when you thought you were so funny? Underneath that: Dewars. A single sentence asked the reader, and consumer, to go through a series of memories and thoughts, to reach a similar conclusion or resolve: Have a drink, don't think about it, you've grown up, and Dewars is for adults, you. What you weren't supposed to be thinking about anymore—parties in the past, your young, stupid behavior—had to be arrived at by each reader through a bunch of moves, little movies in the mind that were stories with attitudes about drunkenness, having a good time, aging, etc. All were arrived at independently but all of them had to come to one punchline, one conclusion—Dewars.

There's the narrative you're writing, and there's the narrative your reader makes from it. There's the time of the story, and there's the time readers take to assimilate the story and add it to theirs, to make it part of their continuing narrative. The Dewars ad accomplished a long story in one short sentence.

When I think about stories and how I write them, when I try to figure out how to tell a story or construct a novel, I wallow for a while in a kind of dumb despair. Thinking about narratives and why I decide or choose, if I'm really choosing, to write one kind rather than another is like thinking the unthinkable. It's impossible: I'm already thinking in stories. One thinks in stories, thinking is a story; "stories are a way to think," I wrote in a story. Narratives are so deeply embedded in how we think and what we think, what we know and how we know it, and in who we are—which narratives about ourselves do we accept as valid and meaningful? do we choose them? how do we choose them?—it's hard to get hold of what stories are. It's hard to see how they function because they are always functioning.

I like it that a floor in a building is called a "story." Architects talk about a building's event, a moment or place in the structure where something happens.

It's one of the questions I have—what has to happen? Is an action required? What is an action? What form does it have to take? A thought? Violence? Resistance? Time passing? Why did the chicken cross the road? To get to the other side. Or is it better: to get to the other side because it was in love with another chicken who was already across the road.

To narrative questions I respond with speculations and explanations. I place them in stories. These speculations and explanations come from somewhere. I may have read them or heard them or experienced them. I may think I'm making them up, but ideas come from somewhere and are based in something. Why I think these, why I give one explanation rather than another, is part of a larger narrative in which I have a small role and out of which I write other parts, or stories.

Theories are explanations, and so are stories. One explains in the same language as the question, one answers the problem with a differently configured problem. Neither a theory nor a story explains completely or adequately, there's always something missing, which gives us the reason to write more of them; but they explain in different forms—stories use characters, generally, in some way, and employ time as an element. There's the time of the story, when it happens. Everything may be a flashback. There's the way and time in which the events are revealed or unraveled, what the reader's told first, second, third. What the reader isn't told, what isn't written, can be the significant lack in a story. All strategies affect the story's meaning, our interpretations of it, since the form of its telling will be part of its meaning.

No matter how one writes characters—not describing them, not assigning them motivation—readers project onto and identify with them. Readers often do most of the work, good actors interpreting a terse script. Even if a writer disdains characters, has ambivalence about what they are and how to construct them, the writer is responsible for having used them at all, having set them, however vaguely or strangely, in a terrain made from words.

In theory, time isn't significant to the unfolding of an argument or to how one understands it. The character of the author of a theory is generally not part of the theory, although there are exceptions—Paul De Man and Heidegger, notable cases in which some people want to make them and their theories the same. In other words, they explain as they do, some insist, in order to defend themselves. This is often said about storytellers.

Both theory and stories are made up things, creations, fictions. One kind of fiction represents arguable truths, as mutable and contextual—interpretations; more terrifying, some theorists assert immutable Truth. The other fiction uses truth as the stuff characters search for, as what can't be found, as what should be found, as human—complex, ambiguous, and contradictory—as the element within the story characters argue about, as a question of right and wrong, which can never be resolved—truth is conflict. Some narratologists say conflict is the essential element in narrative.

Recently I was told that there's turbulence in everything—when you pour milk into a cup of tea, and the tea and milk roil, that's turbulence. I see potential conflict in almost every sentence; placing one word next to another can represent conflict. Language probably emerged from wordless conflict and is riven, every word, with it. This word is not that, for instance.

Conflict may result from the juxtaposition of supposedly different characters—a saint and a sinner; there may be divisions within the same character, or different characters may be representations of different ideas, or conflict emerges from the divergence of warring memories, or from a sentence that contradicts or questions the apparent meaning of a previous sentence. Conflict is an essential part of theorizing, since theories emerge from and depend upon differences from other theories.

There may be imperceptible conflicts, actions, events—I think, thinking is an activity. An emotion may produce an action, be an action, or be a re-action. In some form the writer addresses some kind of event. In some way there is a problem, an event, an action, a thought, an issue, an emotion, to be resolved or left unresolved; there's a problem to be solved, or incapable of solution, a problem engaged or contemplated. There's a kind of adjudicating, whatever the writer does.

The kinds of resolutions one chooses—seemingly chooses—appear as, and at, the ends of one's stories. What one thinks about ends and how one uses them reflects and repeats elements from the great unwritten narrative one is living, much of it unconsciously. Even death isn't much of a closure for a story. Death may end a life in a book, but the reader lives on. Other characters in the story usually do too; the story lives on the page and can be read again.

What really distances stories from theories is that a storyteller is allowed unsubstantiated claims. Theorists are burdened with the problem of proof. I think this is why I make my explanations in the stories I write, rather than as theory. I don't think I can prove anything. Also, I'm not sure what's supposed to be proved. If it's Truth, then that's probably the best reason why I write stories.

Anyone who watches trials on TV sees that truth is always an argument. The lawyers say over and over, we can't find the truth, we're looking for justice. I've begun to think that justice is the subject of most fictions, whatever form they're written in. Again, something is being adjudicated. Somehow all stories are about justice, though I can't prove this.

On the night of June 17, I was watching a Knicks championship game on TV; it was interrupted by a white car driving alone on a six-lane highway. The car was followed by a phalanx of black-and-white police cars. The news commentator, or narrator, told us: O.J. Simpson's inside this car. It's his friend Al Cowlings' white Bronco. O.J.'s got a gun to his head, and he's going to kill himself. The car drove steadily in the middle of the empty highway; the cops followed at what was called a safe distance. It was unbelievably weird and compelling. What was the story? At some point, the TV cut to O.J.'s friend Robert Kardashian reading O.J.'s alleged suicide letter, which ended: Don't remember me this way, as a lost soul. He said he loved Nicole, he didn't do it, and he also said that she had abused him. He was lost, he was guilty, I thought, and he'd written a confession; it contained his defense—that she abused him.

A white car moved along the highway for hours. It carried a man who was a hero to millions. O.J. couldn't turn himself over to the cops. He wanted to see his mother, the narrator said. I started to cry. The car just kept moving. Would he pull the trigger? Was he going to Nicole's grave? I suddenly understood what I was watching—O.J. was making a journey. He needed time and space to achieve a transformation. In order to turn himself over to the cops, he had to become the lost soul he'd written about. He couldn't be the hero, he had to destroy that character. And as much as he needed time, so did many Americans. I used the time to contemplate that he could have done it; it was incredibly sad, like watching a funeral cortege. The hearse was the white Bronco. Because the old O.J. was dead. A mythic figure, he was moving from one world to another, through the underworld, and he had to get to the other side, he had to leave his past life to enter a new, hideously reduced one.

The car turned into O.J.'s driveway. Cowlings parked it at the front door. Cowlings got out, O.J. stayed inside, hidden, there was confusion, Cowlings talked with some police, and then finally O.J. emerged. He was not the same man who began the trip, he was a different man, one who was capable of surrendering. O.J.'s Last Run, the newspapers said.

I've linked O.J. and the white Bronco story with narrative

generally and with specific narratives, the reversal of fortune and the journey, the odyssey. The interpretation of O.J.'s actions and his end is wide open, whether or not he's found guilty. Apart from voyeurism, identification and cultural politics, I'm watching a story whose heart holds questions about justice. That U.S. polls report a great divide between blacks and whites about his guilt is a powerful register of how narratives are read differently, depending upon one's place in the big story. It made me realize that guilt and justice may be independent concepts, operating independently, and that justice may be contending with a notion of collective innocence.

Was there a police plot against O.J.? Is O.J. in a plot with Kardashian? Could he have done it alone, without a plan?

Plot is another great division and question: writers use or don't use plots. Readers want or don't care about plots. People ask me, about the novel I'm writing, What's going to happen? Is there a plot? What's the action? What I want to know, again, is: what is supposed to happen? What kind of event or action? What makes an event worth writing about—a fight with a boss, the search for solitude, a political election, the first time you were called a dirty name—and what form fits the event? And where does plot fit in?

In *Cast in Doubt*, Horace becomes obsessed with Helen, who disappears. First he looks for her in her room just around the harbor from his:

> Sometimes one advances toward a specific destination with not just a sense of purpose and direction, but with a sense of what to expect, and one progresses assured in the knowledge that the world one knows will be as one knows it and has always known it. When I walked to Alicia's house the other week, I knew what I would find there. I did not know of course that her cheeks would be flushed or that she had sung to John, or for him, but I knew where her furniture would be and that her books would be on shelves; I knew how her paintings would be hanging, that there would be flowers in vases, and so on. I knew John might be there, and if he wasn't I knew he would be on another day. One exists with the

sense that life goes on in a regular manner, that one can breathe because one is meant to and air is air, that hello, yá sou, or bonjour will greet one, that fruit and vegetables will be sold where they were sold yesterday—in short, that one can recognize oneself in a recognizable world. And that much of life is ordinary. Even persons in concentration camps were able to adjust, over time, to the most horrific of circumstances, having come to know the routine, which was terrifyingly and mercilessly life as they were compelled by fate to know it, to live it, for however long.

As I walked to Helen's house, I had lost this sense of assurance. I did not know what to expect, which alone unnerved me. I was already unnerved—or nervous—because I didn't understand her disappearance, but when I imagined the consequences of this ignorance, I became confused. I had never even been inside her house. Years ago, when its owner Bliss was still in residence, I visited him there, but that was a long time ago. Much as I tried to envision Helen's house, its contents, and to create it in advance of seeing it, I could not. I simply did not know what awaited me.

Now one may want to interject—part of me does—that I, Horace, sought to feel compassless, to experience the vertiginous highs and lows of the unexpected, having already insisted upon my pleasure in the unknown, having insisted upon how much I needed to invent my life, to make it closer to fiction. But I am a writer and given to such musings. One mustn't believe everything one reads, after all.

Later, he decides to drive his car to search for her in the southern part of Crete:

I drive toward the coast. I don't care to stop or to make a detour. I see no strange encampments along the way. Had I chosen the faster way, I would already have been on the southern coast, quite near to the dot on Helen's map which signified where she had probably gone. But I am not sure if that is the case, or if she had been the one to leave the map lying there, with its mark. Thinking about this is ludicrous, in one way, and confusing in another. I drive, plagued by the uncertainty of it all, and of how this isn't and wasn't like me, to go flying off in pursuit of a mere girl, even one like Helen.

I am discouraged, but hasten to encourage myself to have patience. If Gwen were with me, no doubt she'd caustically remark that I need patience but need more to be the patient. I'd bet the conversation would take such a linguistic turn. I would bet that, were she here to take the bet. I swing around on the road, the road to Mandalay, to somewhere. I am indeed going somewhere.

All he did was drive to another part of Crete to look for her. It's the move, the turn, that makes the book plotted. A journey with a goal. But what if Horace had just stayed home and thought about doing it?

In *Motion Sickness*, the narrator's a traveler; compared with Horace, she's existentially homeless. Her adventures appear undirected, aimless, pointless. Her journey isn't linear; it's circular: she lands up where she started—Paris. The book ends where she began, as if it's all middle. Very middle class, maybe, where the novel originated.

Amsterdam doesn't seem a suitable place for tragedy, but place—the city, for instance—is as much a mental space as a physical one, and its physical boundaries, its history, are much less concise than any term such as "city" might lead one to think. Am I headed for tragedy, I wonder as the cabdriver brings me to the three-generations hotel. And are conversations with strangers necessarily uncanny?

They give me the same room. It still doesn't have a television and I'm embarrassed to ask for one. The breakfasts are also the same, which pleases me enormously. Eat the same thing every day and you won't go mad, also said to me by the friend who insisted upon keeping a diary for the same reason.

I think I understand why so many English plays take place in the restaurants or sitting rooms of hotels. Apart from the cheapness of their production, any aggregate of people, drawn or thrown together and involuntarily in each other's company, poses dramatic possibilities. It's not that you expect anything very fantastic to happen—the American woman named Helen is not going to do a strip in the breakfast room, the Irish guy called Pete is not going to sing an aria just because he feels like it, the German Ulrich will not fall to his knees and confess some terrible crime—there will be no orgy. We are all remarkable for our constraint. If something like that did happen—if Olivier, the Frenchman, exposed himself to me in front of my fellow diners—the course of playwriting would have to be altered, as would the site of the hotel. And I would not now be playing at eating this raisin bun, or *krentebollen*, in the breakfast room. I'd be in a state beyond words, blood racing, or I might be laughing nervously. Olivier merely smiles at me, a sly guarded slash of a grin, throws his book, *Truffaut/Hitchcock*, into his leather satchel, pushes his wire-rimmed glasses up onto the bridge of his nose and strides past me, brushing against my arm ever so slightly. Why do I feel I've seen this scene before?

And will I end up in bed with him? Is my life as predictable as it sometimes appears?

Some readers felt the lack of a scheme or plot, saw no reason for her to travel, some tried to find a reason, for some there was no reason to read on. I did supply a coy subplot—a character who may be a spy appears everywhere—but I didn't make him central. His surprising presence was supposed to lie there, a layer in the book, something for readers to play with. In this way writing's geological, reading's archaeological.

If I'd written that the unnamed narrator was adopted, and searching for her real mother or father, and her journey took her all those places to find one of them or both, it might've appealed to some readers. It might have supplied a reason to read the book.

What is the point in reading? Or in writing? A plot, or a scheme, gives a reason, I suppose. Plots seem to me about rationality, direction, and goals. A plotted novel written by Patricia Highsmith, about guilt and the irrational, has a mercenary murderer like Ripley acting rationally. She emphasizes his orderliness—Ripley's nothing if not rational. He has clever reasons for everything and follows a stringent regime in executing his executions. Presumably that's why he's never caught. Except I think it's because he doesn't experience guilt, and doesn't want to be caught, so he doesn't leave clues. Though Highsmith plots his every move, every Ripley action or thought is fraught, open to a reader's anxiety. Ripley's reasoning is an open, anxious question. Highsmith uses rationality and plots to explore the irrational and unplotted.

If you don't need a plot, what does that mean? I like stories with plots. I like ones that don't have them. I sometimes find plots where they may not be, which means that as a reader I invent reasons for why something does or doesn't happen. As a writer, I question the need for goals or directions, for specific outcomes based on specific actions or events. Since the unconscious and the irrational guide us as much as the conscious and rational, I have trouble determining plots. To me there are many, many reasons why things happen or don't, and I'm concerned about over-emphasizing one or two. Also, plot seems a way of setting limits— to control the meaning of a story. It can set out a "because" and a "therefore." That can be a trick, too, a writer's ruse, and therefore not a therefore at all.

These are all questions. As a reader I want pleasure, and as a writer I want to provide pleasure—we read for pleasure. But pleasure comes in many forms—some plotted, some not. There's no pleasure, release, without frustration. There's pleasure from pain. Which might make reading and writing sadomasochistic. How much frustration is permissible? How are forms frustrating and why? Why do some of us need to feel there's a goal?

In *Cast in Doubt*, Gwen thinks that Horace wanted to find his name in Helen's diary, not find Helen, not find himself, just his name. Each of us writing is invested in naming, designating, marking, representing, making inclusions and exclusions. Each of us reading wants to find ourselves in books in some way, in different ways, some very abstract. How much of what we do or find is already determined or how much choice we have in what we find or do or the way we do it—those are implicit elements in any story, affecting the way one writes it or reads it.

As writers our desires and our limits enter our stories, dressed up as events and characters; as readers, through our desires and limits, we take up these events and characters, or their lack, and make them ours, or don't. The most bedeviling question for writers, I think, is whether any of us can turn our unconscious and conscious desires and our historically and psychologically determined limits, our necessities, into virtues, and whether our vices can become our books' virtues.

1995

22. Like Rockets and Television II

Edie Sedgwick using the only telephone in the Factory

The summer of 1993, when the Velvet Underground regrouped, for a minute, some of Stephen Shore's photographs of the Velvets appeared in an English magazine. An editor from an English publishing house, Pavilion, wanted Shore to do a book of them. The editor asked Shore if he knew a writer. Two weeks before— Stephen and I were teaching in an MFA program—I told Stephen that the last time I'd seen him was in 1967 at a party in his parents' apartment. Warhol was there. I think I remember seeing him. Then I described to Stephen what his parents' apartment looked like and how and where he was standing. Stephen didn't remember me. He didn't know my writing. But I had remembered what he and things looked like then, had a picture in my mind, like a photograph, and that impressed him, he said. He asked me to be the writer.

I started by interviewing Stephen, whose memory, he claimed, wasn't great. We looked at his pictures together and talked; we had five sessions. Then I decided to interview other people associated with the Factory, some of whom I knew. I researched Warhol's films and the art he made then and earlier, I looked up dates and when works first appeared and where, details I hate doing, read what was written about Warhol and his work at the time, captioned all the pictures, more details I hate, and then wrote an essay about Warhol and the Factory.

I realized I was doing history, involved, to some extent, in the growing Warhol corpus, his body of work, his body and other bodies, and his corpse—after an important artist's death, various institutions and people begin to close in, to gather information, to buy work, to sell it, to memorialize, capitalize, to assert influence, to shape interpretation, etc. Oddly enough, sometimes the people closest to the artist are not the best interpreters. I'm reminded of the temporary fate of Chaucer, whose pupil John Lydgate was, for about 100 to 200 years after Chaucer's death, considered a greater poet. Lydgate is thought to have hurt the reputation of Chaucer's poetry because he dropped the pronunciation of the final e from Chaucer's lines.

Allowed 30,000 words, including captions, for 200 photographs,

I decided to give most of the words to Stephen and the people who'd been part of the Factory. My method involved meeting with them, if I could, and showing them xeroxes of 200 pictures. I asked questions, taped everything, tried to get them to identify others in the pictures, let the pictures function as aides-memoires. Sometimes I talked to people over the phone; sometimes I mailed them xeroxes of pictures, then talked with them over the phone.

I decided to interview only those people in Stephen's photographs. That was a self-imposed limit. I met with Taylor Mead and then found out he wasn't in any of Stephen's photographs. Stephen was there the two years that Taylor Mead was out of the picture. So I used a quote from Mead as one of the epigraphs to my introduction.

"Andy was difficult. I mean, it was great to be with him. He was cheap and impossible some days. I consider him a genius, I guess. Whatever that means." — Taylor Mead[1]

I couldn't find Chuck Wein. I phoned everywhere, even a horse breeding establishment that I was told he might still work for. Brigid Berlin wouldn't talk to me. I got her on the phone. But she said, Oh no; then I discovered she'd been fired or had left the Warhol Foundation, only days before. Lou Reed refused to be interviewed, his assistant said; I thought about using his lyrics, but knew that would become a nightmare. The Velvets had split up again, etc.

The photographs were the first frame. Through them I excluded or included possible speakers for the book. And I used the photographs as something to talk about.

The interview format was another frame. How did I frame my questions? Why did I ask what I asked? In interviews, in doing history through interviews, one relies on experience and memory, rather than on already written texts — after all, history is what is written, recorded — and even if they contest one another, written texts have the status of history. But in trying to get history, in trying to encourage a series of words, or images, to narrate two

1 Unless noted otherwise, all quotes are from LT's interviews or essay, "Like Rockets and Television," first published in *The Velvet Years: Andy Warhol and the Factory 1965–1967* (London: Pavilion, 1995).

years, 1965–1967, of the Factory and to add to the Warhol story, I became one of those choosing what gets written down. That felt ominous.

It's why I decided not to do an overview or to paraphrase but to present most of the material in the interviewees' words. Reading interview after interview is tedious, so I edited myself out and presented the interviews as stories and thoughts, as prose narratives in the speakers' voices. Conversations are unwieldy and fragmented. I had to edit a lot; I couldn't use hundreds of pages of material. I had to select what I thought was most important, most compelling, for a kind of record that was already incomplete, reduced or preselected. If several people agreed about something, for example, I might have only one of them say it in their section. Sometimes there was considerable overlap. Sometimes that seemed important to indicate.

At the very end, Stephen reduced the number of photographs; the layout was too crowded. The design changed, and even more words had to be cut. There's an alternative universe, another history or histories, that could be culled from what is edited out. It could be called "the deleted." Some of the deleted stories and thoughts that would have been in *The Velvet Years* are:

"Danny Fields said, I can't believe we all had crushes on Lou. But he was sexy. Dark, sullen. He was pleasant enough to me. We used to go to transvestite after-hours bars and stay up drinking coffee to 4, 8, 10 in the morning. He had stuff to say, the Delmore Schwartz background, he was well read in a certain kind of literature. I would talk to people about things. That's what I remember, substance."—Donald Lyons

"Edie thought Andy would be her ticket to film stardom, that she'd be the focus forever of Andy and the Factory's interest. She'd be the permanent pop girl. She didn't realize that the flux was very furious at the Factory; so Edie was there, then we came along, not wishing to be the pop girl of '66, or anything else. We were there because Andy wanted to put a show together, wanted us to be the band. It didn't impinge on anything else, as far as we were concerned; he never asked us to assist in making silkscreens, he never asked us to give him ideas for his paintings. We just played music and were in the photographs. Edie got very upset, when all of a sudden Andy's interest seemed to turn to the show and us — what was her role going to be in the show? Nothing, in particular. She could dance if she liked. If you wanted to work the projectors, work the projectors. Edie wasn't happy with that. After we arrived, official, she more or less departed officially, and fell in with the Dylan camp disastrously." — Sterling Morrison

"I never understood what all the excitement was about the silver toilet. It seemed to create such an incredible effect. I never quite got it. I think it was also because I'd been in a million lofts, so it all seemed a little bit old West Village stuff. The West Village was full of photographers. Every beautiful long, leggy thing was invited up to someone's studio, to have some sort of photograph taken, so it felt a little bit like that." — Pat Hartley

"The whole Factory, every evening, would go to some restaurant, some event. We'd go to the Ginger Man, where Edie had an account; she'd pick up the bill. Nothing to eat during the day except milkshakes, junk food, then we'd go out and, WOW, steaks, hamburgers, dessert. Everybody would order a dessert which nobody would eat, except Edie. She would eat everybody's dessert. Thin as a rail, but she would eat like a horse. Three, four desserts. I think Barbara Rubin said she learned how to lose weight from Edie, when they met in upstate New York, wherever this mental home was where they were incarcerated—I think that's how Barbara introduced Edie to Andy. They used to eat, and she would throw up. Bulimic, exactly." — John Cale

"SYNDROMES POP AT DELMONICO'S: Andy Warhol and His Gang Meet the Psychiatrist—The New York Society for Clinical Psychiatry survived an invasion . . . billed as an evening's entertainment for the psychiatry society's 43rd annual dinner at Delmonico's Hotel . . . 'I suppose you could call this gathering a spontaneous eruption of the id,' said Dr. Alfred Lilienthal. 'Warhol's message is one of super-reality,' said another. 'Why are they exposing us to these nuts?' a third asked. 'But don't quote me.' . . . The act really came into its own midway through the dinner when the Velvet Underground swung into action . . . Guests stream[ed] out. 'Put it down as decadent Dada,' said one. 'It was ridiculous, painful,' said Dr. Harry Weinstock. 'It seemed like a whole prison ward had escaped.' " —Grace Glueck, *New York Times*, 1/14/66. (Glueck was to have been the sole exception to my rule about not including people who weren't in Stephen's photographs.)

"Andy and I talked about movies. He liked Doris Day, superficial Hollywood movies, certain European avant-garde films. Jacques Demy. Extravagant Hollywood movies. He might have liked *Vertigo*, not because it was Hitchcock, but because it was a kind of lurid, insane display of personality, or image." —Donald Lyons

"Last time I saw Danny Williams was when Lou had hepatitis, and I had to do the honors of the singing because we were booked into Poor Richard's in Chicago. I sang from the piano, and drew this review— 'Flowers of Evil are in Full Bloom' at Poor Richard's. I heard this thumping going on in the middle of the set. I looked up from the piano into the dark. Paul Morrissey was out there, where the projector was, with Danny. It was something that happened at every gig, like clockwork. Paul and Danny had their arms around each other's throats, and they were like leaning over the parapet and they were punching each other, about whoever could get to the extension cord first. That's what they were fighting over, the bloody extension cord." —John Cale

"Andy didn't live with his mother, Andy's mother lived with him. She moved in on him. They were Old World. My family's like that too. Like I live near where my mother was born, right in this neighborhood [Poughkeepsie, N.Y.]. The church I was baptized in was in this neighborhood. My mother still lives here. Linich is Prussian. And on one side my father is Prussian and Junker, both Germanic. My mother is Italian, Naples and Sicily. I'm the Central European. The Axis powers. See, I had trouble with that when I was a child. People used to call me Nazi when I was a kid. Like I was the actual enemy. I was born in 1940. I was the enemy kid." — Billy Name (Billy Linich)

I didn't represent one point of view, except in my introductory essay, where I wrote some of what I think about Warhol and his work. In doing the interviews, and of course my essay, I had to recognize and occasionally assert my biases. I made claims: Warhol as anarchic artist and filmmaker, as scenemaker, as queer social critic, as irreverent and reverent, as a shopper, a scandal, a culture vulture, a dissonant, as a multifaceted, troubling voice, and more.

I functioned as an art critic and interpreted "*Thirteen Most Wanted Men*:"

In 1964, Philip Johnson, the architect, asked Warhol to decorate the New York State Pavilion for the World's Fair building which Johnson had designed. Warhol produced *Thirteen Most Wanted Men*, meant to grace the outside of the building—thirteen criminals in profile and full face. Decoration for a state building. The image was rejected, as might have been expected and intended; then Warhol proposed a replacement—cover the building with images of Robert Moses, the World's Fair director. This sweetly perverse reversal of positions was also rejected. In the end Warhol painted over *Thirteen Most Wanted Men* in his signature aluminum/silver paint. The wanted men obscured, made obscene, they were set against the state, or under it, as a palimpsest. They were the literal underworld of the state, a physical layer residing in the state.

It's an uncanny rebellion. Max Weber defined the state as that institution alone legitimated to kill. Some of the Most Wanted Men must have committed murder, a practice reserved for the state. So the preserve of art and the preserve of the state met on the surface of the building and had a silvered fate, were a turn of events, like that which the flip of a coin might produce, as flip as a coin flip, those changed positions or fates. *Most Wanted Men*'s other provocation is sexual, challenging the State with an outlaw, unspeakable love, homosexuality, to haunt it as underbelly. Warhol, queer-American, gives new meaning to the phrase "self-made man." A self made into any man, bad, good, as random an end as the flip of that coin.

*

I presented Warhol as productive, contradictory, a man whose thinking and making continues to shape the present, whose work and life confounds most categories, most oppositions. Along with other leading figures of the sixties, there was an attempt made on his life. It failed, but it changed him and the Factory radically. In a curious way Warhol's place as a cultural leader, and the way the Factory was a parallel world to the larger world, is hinted at through the mimickry of the assassination attempt. It was that kind of time.

Another bias was to present the Factory people I talked with not as survivors—of Warhol, of the sixties, of the Factory. And to present the Factory not as a desperate place of no return, where everyone died and everyone else left hung on, or were losers, even beautiful ones. Life is led and goes on in all sorts of ways. I was interested in the living, and the living can be interviewed.

"Experience is at once always already an interpretation and something that needs to be interpreted." — Joan Scott[2]

"An interview's result is evidence and reason why no characterization or generalization of Warhol and the Factory is true enough, accurate enough, or adequate, or entirely convincing. No interview result is untroubled by memory or subjectivity or desire or experience."

Paul Morrissey told me there were no parties at the Factory, maybe two, in all the time he worked with Andy; the existence of the parties was just media hype. Others told me that there were parties all the time. For some people, two's a crowd.

The edited interviews stand as fragments, bits and pieces, increments, meant to be incremental, meant to add to other texts. A silent interrogator is eliciting or urging responses. Among many questions, I was interested in how Catholic the Factory was and in Warhol's catholicism, in both senses. I wanted to know how class

1. Joan Scott, "The Evidence of Experience," *Critical Inquiry* (Summer 1991): p. 797.

operated at the Factory, since class divisions are evident in his films, such as *Bike Boy*, as well as in his choice of objects to frame. In a country that pretends class isn't a problem, Warhol was class conscious. He had a class act.

People answered the questions or parts or didn't. Being the interviewer is as weird as being the interviewee. There's nothing neutral about either position. It's a set up, asking questions, getting answers, an exchange with agendas, and both sides usually have one or several. Sometimes I lost myself in the answers and forgot why I had asked the question. I asked leading questions. Maybe all questions are leading—is one really disinterested in the answers? Especially when one is writing a history, and one has biases, implicit and explicit. And even the words that weren't my words became "my material" to shape, from which to construct narratives, partial histories.

No one provided the total story, no one could, there isn't one, no one told me everything, although Danny Fields' memory was so acute, it seemed as if he could. The total picture couldn't fit within one frame, each frame is a character, with all of that character's complexity. All the characters have different viewpoints, and each augments the others, or maybe detracts, but unlike the metaphorical or real jigsaw puzzle one hopes to finish, there are pieces missing. That's a given. And everyone would want a different finished puzzle anyway, a puzzle specific to each one of them, where each would be a little more central in and to the completed, but always incomplete, composition.

"In the end, reality will always remain unknowable." —Freud[3]

Doing the project I was doing, trying to get at what happened, what the Factory was like, how people saw the times and themselves and Warhol, I felt I was living Freud's dictum. It was incontrovertible.

"Is the Factory, now that it's gone, just a place, a physical space, or an historical space, is it a mental space, or even a frame of mind?"

3. Freud, *Outline of Psychoanalysis*, Standard Edition p. 106.

What would be a Factory frame of mind? Does anyone still have it? Jonas Mekas commented, and I paraphrase, that while he thought Warhol's films were unique, he thought what Warhol had started would continue. There would be more Factories. But now he realizes that wasn't true. It was unique too.

"The Factory itself was a frame, including, excluding. It was a part of the Sixties 'counterculture,' but counter to much of that too. Maybe Warhol's Factory was counterculture, not as straight, more on the couch than on the bus or road."

What is the Factory now; what will we make of it, what purposes will it serve, how will it be interpreted, what will we make it be?

What are these photographs, now? They can't be taken at face value. They are art objects, visual objects. They are places or spaces, with history, holding history, about a historical moment, but how are pictures history? When is a photograph a historical document? What does it need to document? Do famous people in a photograph make it historical? Can any photograph, which is necessarily of the past, claim to be part of a history?

Pictures are apposite to, and analogues to, the problems of history. They need interpretation. They are not transparent. They don't control meaning, they don't limit meaning, they allow for meanings, they can be ambiguous, they ask to be decoded, they will be projected into and onto. They can be evidence—such as, Warhol is behind the camera; so he shot his films. Or, there was only one telephone in the Factory on 47th Street. But these "pictorial facts" can be contested; the former is. By citing or writing about them, one engages in determining their meanings and their value. Photographs aren't conclusions or necessarily conclusive.

What was I showing to the people I interviewed?

Someone I know said that when he saw photographs of the Factory, when he was a teenager, they were like rock 'n' roll to him. They gave him the same kind of feeling.

The Chelsea Girls recently played at the Film Forum in New York. A friend who'd only read about the Factory and people like Nico and seen the pictures was amazed by it. *The Chelsea Girls* was very different from what he expected. What was that?

I asked. He hadn't expected that it would be sad.

As I worked, I asked myself, a little plagued: When one studies history, when one investigates memory and experience, when one studies other people's pasts, when one looks at photographs, what is one looking for? And, when doing something like this, how is one in the present? How is the past coterminous with the present, and how is it not? What is one's attachment to the past in the present? And why that past and not another? How is the present changed by the study of history, by one's absorption in even a recently past moment?

I thought of a Borges-like story in which a character, like me, becomes consumed with a year—let's say 1965. Here it is 1995, all I want to do is find out about 1965. It becomes more and more urgent to me. I want to know everything. Everything takes up more of my time than I have in 1995. Many more days of time, oddly enough, than there are in 1995, and in 1965, because to study as many facets as I can of 1965, I must necessarily live that earlier year in a way that I don't live the present. I would want to know what was happening everywhere else and in the lives of others, whom I don't know, with the kind of intensity and attention I reserve for friends. That takes time and energy. I would be trying to encompass time in a way that one does not live time. Studying even one day in 1965 would take more time than twenty-four hours in 1995, maybe it'd take a year.

"I feel I'm very much part of my times, of my culture, as much a part of it as rockets and television."—Andy Warhol[4]

Writing this book sometimes seemed anti-Warhollian. Warhol was very much in his time, of it, in a present, his present, which became part of other peoples' lives, their present. He made the present as dense as history. He chose to make art and films from the present moment and instantly made the present into history. When you think about *A: A Novel*, Warhol taping and documenting

4. Gretchen Berg, interview with Warhol, in *Cahiers du Cinema* (English), (May 1967).

twenty-four hours in the life of Ondine, you realize he's making history of and in the present tense. He's recording, preserving — preserving the present — archiving, and even extending present time, which he did again and again, with real-time films and serial images. Maybe Warhol's sense of time was Augustinian. Maybe my project wasn't completely anti-Warhollian.

Of all the comments made about Warhol, one of the most intriguing was: He asked other people for ideas. Henry Geldzahler, Gordon Baldwin, and others told me he asked people for ideas. Or they said he said, Tell me what to do. It seemed important but hard to figure out, another curious Warhollian element. Gordon Baldwin said: "It's something people haven't noted very much."[5] How does one note or emphasize it? He wasn't interested in being the originator of the idea; he wasn't interested in the origin of the idea, where it came from or who it came from. It's easy to talk now in terms of appropriation — he appropriated images, he appropriated ideas — but how does one interpret, "Tell me what to do?" What is its meaning? It can be used as evidence by those who think Warhol is "unoriginal." Stephen Shore thought he did it to include other people in his work, to keep people around. Psychoanalytically, one could think about symbiosis, about his relationship to his mother — maybe he's saying, Tell me what to do, Mommy, and keeping her with him. It may entail Oedipal issues, sadomasochism, and narcissism, too. It's also about a human exchange, with the idea as currency, as a kind of money, which also meant something to Warhol. He even made paintings of it.

Ultimately, "tell me what to do" made me wonder what an idea was. The history of art, to name one history, is filled with notions about ideas: whose idea was it, who did it first, where did it start, who influenced whom, with ideas about ideas as forms. In the work of Warhol the status of the idea — its relevance, its origin, and its originality — is a question. The difficulty about what an idea is is in the work, how something like an appropriated image

5. In *The Velvet Years*.

functions apart from and as part of its origin. Someone who borrows ideas likes borrowed ideas.

I thought about it in three ways:

One, he worked all the time, everyone said that, he never stopped making things, so for him maybe an idea is different from its execution, or maybe an idea doesn't exist until it's made; maybe he objected to something's being "just an idea."

Two, if you think of the frame, a social frame expanding and contracting, if you see Warhol inside a culture, a culture he feels part of, like rockets and television, then maybe the idea is an idea precisely because it circulates, is available, not because it's hard to find or that it should have to be found at all. What is an unrealized idea? Is it still an idea or only just an idea—useless? Would anyone have realized these ideas if Warhol hadn't? Was it in Warhol's mind to make every idea into work?

Three, hasn't Warhol himself become a borrowed idea? Hasn't he become an idea? I've borrowed him and his work to write about, to use for my own ends and to organize my "own" borrowed ideas.

As for ends, ideas, and borrowings: on Sunday, April 23, Billy Name and Callie Angell went to the film set of *I Shot Andy Warhol*, to be produced by Tom Kalin and Christine Vachon and directed by Mary Harron. They wanted Billy Name to critique the set, a re-creation of the silver factory. They wanted to know if they got it right.[6]

1995

6. On April 24, 1995, I was told by Callie Angell that this didn't happen on April 23. Instead, on the 24th Billy Name went to the set, not only to critique it but also to shoot some Warhol-like Screen Tests of people aspiring to be extras, or Factory people, for it.

23. Past Shock

Any contemporary story about the past or even the present acts like a fairy tale, telling us about ourselves through imagined, extreme analogies. Historical reconstructions reveal us looking back in a hall of mirrors. *I Shot Andy Warhol*, directed by Mary Harron, is complicated in its depiction of a recent history, complex in its aims and ambitions, and in its filmic conception and production. It's complicated to watch, especially if you lived through the period it represents or wandered through some of its scenes.

Using or producing Warhol history—any history—is a tender, touchy project, troublingly familiar. A weight called responsibility hangs over anyone who traffics in history. If one accepts the role of the critic, one should first be self-critical. If one uses history, one should historicize oneself. These are daunting, half-possible tasks—pulling yourself out of your thoughts while in them.

Since a return to the past is impossible, a fantasy, what does it mean to be faithful to history? Can we only recognize and record the past as a problem for the present in the present? *I Shot Andy Warhol* is seen through a prism of positions, when, a) one already has ideas about Warhol, b) not much information about him or the period, and/or c) did or didn't live through it. A dramatic, vivid, uneasy movie, it leaves traces, unsettles, produces shocks of recognition and misrecognition.

After a packed press screening, I shared a cab with three friends. One said: Andy seemed pretty nice. One responded: I thought he was disgusting. The other listened. The friend who thought Warhol seemed nice in the movie likes Warhol's work; the friend who thought he was disgusting hates it, him. Like most things, the movie will most likely confirm already-received ideas and opinions, while threatening others.

In Michel Auder's 1971 video, *Chelsea Girls*, Viva (Susan Hoffman), a Warhol star, and Brigid Polk (Brigid Berlin) are filmed in the Hotel Chelsea, talking to Warhol over the phone. Warhol doesn't know he's being audiotaped. Auder's video is a behind-the-scene, surreptitious glance at Warhol. Everyone in it seems coy and naive, simultaneously, which might be the effect of *video verité*. Is there ever a "real" Warhol lurking, Andy without preconceptions? What's *verité* anyway?

Harron's Warhol is the enigmatic, charismatic group leader. In a memorably charged, discomforting scene, he's seated on a couch at a party, surrounded by four women vying for his attention, his anything. Max Weber never said charismatic leaders were nice. Deeply curious creatures, they're concocted of unfailing and dubious charm; they're disturbing figures, who are often disturbed. Jared Harris's Warhol is a blend of ambiguities—passivity, playfulness, cruelty, sweetness, indifference. Lili Taylor plays Valerie Solanas as intelligent, edgy, wry; like the others, she wants to get close to him, wants something from him—in her case, to produce her play.

At the Factory and in Harron's movie, Warhol's the center. He's the half-empty or half-full glass, matter for projection. Watching *I Shot Andy Warhol* is also made from projections. On the cinematic couch, each of us is a case of identification or disidentification. Once Warhol enters the movie, the narrative, like Solanas, is swayed and changed by his presence. This may be my projection. And my reading of the title *I Shot Andy Warhol* may also be. The title generates questions about the movie's attitude toward Warhol that may have been unintended and unthought; it carries the all-too-prevalent ambivalence and cynicism about Warhol and his near-death.

Based on a script by Harron and Dan Minahan, *I Shot Andy Warhol* reconstructs and plunders history, but not as documentary. History conforms to the rules of narrative fiction. It's easy to jerk reflexively to a recreation, to its not being what it was, really. I kept thinking: I don't know what it was. Harron's decision to portray Solanas in a fiction and as a fictional character signifies her understanding of the problem of "finding Solanas." The real Warhol, the real Solanas are the wrong things to look for. Why do we look anyway?

Recently there were three exhibitions in Soho, all taking historical stock: at Exit Art/The First World, curated by Brian Wallis, "Counterculture: Alternative Information from the Underground Press to the Internet"; at the Drawing Center, "Cultural Economies: Histories from the Alternative Arts Movement, NYC," curated by Julie Ault of Group Material; and at Artists Space, "Mr. Dead & Mrs. Free: The History of Squat Theater," curated by Eva Buchmuller, Claudia Gould, and Anna Koos. Covering work from the '60s to the mid-'80s, the shows are evidence of a determined, backward glance, of the desire to collect and study cultures and subcultures that have disappeared or seem to have. Is it coherence we're searching for, attested to by past strategies or movements, not necessarily recognized at the time as movements or as coherent? What are the uses of history? To turn pieces into wholes, most especially when a present seems splintered?

In *I Shot Andy Warhol*, the spectacle of the '60s runs across the screen, scenes seen through the lens of the '90s, and it's a wild, scary juxtaposition. Solanas, writer, lesbian, feminist who turned tricks, a paranoid who was ill before her introduction to Warhol, becomes the entryway into that difficult, turbulent time, while the Factory is a microcosm for a society and culture in revolt and convulsion.

The chaos of change in the '60s, its sexual openness and its outlaws, finds a place in the movie's *mises-en-scènes*: the Factory party, the backroom at Max's, the New York diner scenes. The reenactments reminded me of late, strange nights and strange places. The tableaux seemed superimposed, out of alignment, but they jarred memory from sleep and were close enough, disconcerting. They felt like archaeological sites; I was at a cinematic excavation. A weird sense of distended space and time, of continuities and discontinuities, connections and disconnections, multiplied the movie's complexity.

We're history's orphans, shaped by it, abandoned by it, searching ironically for our birth parents. Through our representations of what's no longer available, we discover our hunger for what's missed, lost. Idealized or demonized, there are our reflections, our images, on flat surfaces. Valerie Solanas, representative of an anguished, vital time in American history, is a kind of access to the period, a sad way to Warhol and the fantasy and possibilities of a now-glamorous lost moment. (Her *Scum Manfesto*, an excoriating, anti-male tract, is definitely symptomatic of the time.) The elusive, brilliant Warhol encountered Valerie Solanas, an extremely disturbed, ambitious, thwarted, talented woman. Her failure to thrive in his, or any, environment turned their meeting into a tragic collision. In all its perplexing, telling, fraught overdeterminations, that crash is a product of history, made in and about America.

1996

24. The Matisse Pages from Madame Realism's Diary

October 12: Staying home, not returning telephone calls, reading, watching TV; am somewhat edgy, anticipating terrible news. Election returns. All of NYC holding its collective breath. Am turning into myself or upon myself, or anyway inward, like hibernating bear, if bears do turn inward. But eager to go out at night, more like a vampire, current metaphorical rage, than a bear, which would be cumbersome. Reading the newspaper closely. Should arrange for ticket to Matisse show. Resent need to plan. Would like to stroll in and see it, alone. Reminds me of that line in Preston Sturges's *The Palm Beach Story*, when train porter, who was tipped just ten cents by Claudette Colbert's companion, tells Joel McCrea that Colbert's "alone but she don't know she's alone." Don't want to go and yet would like to see it. Is it that Matisse's "genius," proclaimed throughout the land, along with precious attention to his wives and mistresses, his taste in food, drink, and habitats, forces one to engage in a joke at one's own expense? Entry into show will be entry into joke, whose punchline is the trivialization of one's existence. Or is this only anticipatory anxiety, future fear of wounded narcissism? Which reminds me of a Dutch idiom, *Je bent de sigaar*, which means, literally, you are the cigar, but which means, idiomatically, you are the butt of the joke. Might write a book called *The Idiom*.

October 18: Dinner at Indian restaurant. Ordering dishes becomes more complicated when sharing food appears indicative of character, nebulous but damning. Conversation about whether one is or is not willing to visit Matisse show because of nauseating promo. Talk of Matisse and Madonna's *Sex*, encouraging inane puns about overexposure. Easier to buy *Sex* than have it, someone says. One artist announces he isn't going to Matisse, couldn't be bothered. I question if not going, because of crowds or cultural fetishization, is foolish; he demurs, explaining position more fully. I feel similarly, I tell him, but would not act on it, since it was a part of me I resisted and distrusted. Then repeat what my father used to intone when I was a child: "Si and Hi went to the circus. Si got hit with a rolling pin. Si said to Hi, Let's get even with the circus. We'll buy two tickets and we won't go in." All looked at me strangely. What nursery rhymes did they learn, I wonder?

October 31: Halloween. Venture out even though once pledged never again, after having been hit with egg. Downtown filled with wanderers in garish makeup, though city silent as a communal grave; streets giant cemeteries with souls wandering about in the eerie quiet costumed as hatchet murderers, movie stars, animals. Our heathen carnival. Others standing near me pelted with eggs that rain down from above; I am unscathed. Small miracles abound. Evening amazing for the hush; characters dressed as TVs, other objects, but even masked no one seems dangerous. Most amazing of all, no one dressed as Matisse.

November 3: Raining. Election Day. Radio says rain is bad for the Democrats. Why? Statements like that annoying, precisely because one remembers them. Decide to do Matisse before or after voting. Lines will be long everywhere. Relatively small crowds at MOMA, I'm told by two guards who regard us all with a trying mixture of curiosity, revulsion, and boredom; those compelled to watch thousands of people every day must have a debased view of life. As I walk around imagine being incorporated into M's diary, the auto/biographical emphasized by chronological design/order of installation. Crowd's comments: "He likes oranges." "He likes pots."

Matisse likes reading women, as well as undressed women, even partially undressed readers. But is "like" the right word? Fascination with women reading is a vast subject, not his but art's. Eyes averted, inaccessible, in another world, cerebral, unavailable, "givers of life" representing world/life before one was given life, perhaps. Funny to look at, really; thoughts about oblivion cluster mentally. Reference to 19th-century women being "given" literacy. Question: Is this image another woman(liness) as masquerade? A study of self-consciousness or of self into consciousness? Will never mail postcard of a woman reading now without ambivalence.

What are goldfish, apart from the obvious—small orange penises. What is obviousness? What's simple/clear about M's having painted penises, if he did, in goldfish bowls, and elsewhere, over and over again? A friend tells me there's an essay about the goldfish whose point is, because M had red hair, goldfish are Matisse. Is that "le penis, c'est moi?" Hectic being in this goldfish bowl gazing at goldfish and nudes. In thrall to M's lurid, hedonistic, frozen Moroccan moments, his plunge into cultural/sexual dubiousness, his pleasuring in foreign exoticism. Domestic exoticism, the nudes in his studio, who became an abiding, enduring home away from home (wife and children) he left behind in Paris after World War I.

M's "other" landscape, land as body, bodies of land, bodies to be landed on; Woman, not alone his vanishing point, though his Odalisques with their legs spread wide proclaim absence makes the art. Can't help punning. Actually am a pun, which most don't get. You don't understand me/the married man's joke. M was married: remember that, I tell myself, as I look at "Conversation." Man stands on one side, woman on the other, a relationship on two planes separated by a window. G.K. Chesterton: "For views I look out the window. My opinions I keep to myself."

Lusty old M, filled with blood lust and sucking on blood oranges. Oranges and orange goldfish. Matisse paints himself seated, immobile before the sensual life he sets down on canvas. The delicious meal he serves up for himself, memorializes; he lets nothing come in his way, the objects he wants in front of him he places there, the world at the foot of his easel, his palette, his plate. M a pleasure seeker. His paintings beautiful, pleasurable. Their object, no doubt, pleasure. He wants "purity, serenity," but pleasure is not, as love is not, "pure," always messy, an admixture. How does one know pleasure? Pleasure seeks an object. Everything has an object; everything is an object. Sometimes an abject object, which is, it seems to me, the more I think about the Moroccan paintings, an appropriate idea. But what are the ideas one has when thinking about M's work? Is pleasure an idea when looking at a painting?

Two Italian men stand near, murmuring in that wonderful tongue, gazing with me at *Anemones in an Earthenware Vase* (1924). Italians walk away. Wearing red bandannas, like Matisse's Gypsies, and Levi's 501s. Jean jackets read: "Live the Legend."

Disdain M's dancers, dance to represent Life, Dance of Life. Uncomplicated overexuberance. Degas's dancers, at least, sometimes narcissistic, distracted, bored. M's dancers, like bad art, tired metaphors. Remind me of movies that try to be artful, so incorporate "art," have it on walls or include dialogue about art, especially set in a gallery. Matisse seats himself before the dance of life. One painting teacher I studied with said never sit while painting because it was lazy and you were at work.

On line to bathroom someone says, I think—or did I read it or dream it?—"M's trying to find the essence under the modernist illusion." Essence *is* modernist illusion.

An older man with beard keeps turning up in front of me. His head bent low, he cranes his neck to see the work on the walls, then hurries on, and reappears, bent down, worried, harried, deeply depressed. Seems to be an artist struck dumb by the Master. Taking to heart the greatness, the genius, of Matisse.

Am moving ahead of the crowd as much as possible and occasionally have chance to stand in front of a picture alone, but just for a brief moment. All of us here, trying to get a look at these paintings, even for a second and in some discomfort, brings to mind strongly the genius business, which keeps crossing me up.

Why? Because finally I am looking at the work through that frame more than at/through anything else. So it's already seen, observed, served up and serving. What does it serve, ideologically, aesthetically, economically, etc., to foster the myth of genius? Easier to understand it ideologically, than, say, psychologically, except as cultural version of master/slave condition.

Think later and more about this exhibition in relation to Russian Constructivist show at Guggenheim, its emphasis on the many developing a collective visual language. One looks at or views (how is viewing different from looking? less invested, disinterested, disinvented?) that work differently, I think, because of context, which provokes/produces different thoughts from Matisse show. With its biographical trajectory can't stop being aware of Matisse the man, and am not interested in him.

Took longer to vote than to go through exhibition. Meet a friend on line. Discuss election and Matisse. Talk about pleasure and Matisse, to indulge one's pleasures, which pleasures at what time, and the hope for the man from Hope—to have more citizen pleasure.

Drink coffee while waiting. Hot coffee a pleasure. Some pleasures one has no guilt about. What makes it pleasurable, if/when it is, to look at art? Economic explanation not sufficient. Clinton wins; but Perot does pretty well, since it pays to advertise, for one thing, and he is such a cute, paranoid critter. More people vote this year than in the past six elections, but still not many more than half the eligible. Commentators keep saying it's the end of cynicism, which bothers me as much as emphasis on male genius. Is doubt unhealthy? Is the American myth/dream of change and hope like the myth of genius? Serving different or same ends? Still, an avowed skeptic is not thrown off course so easily.

1993

25. In Memoriam: Craig Owens

It took me a few weeks to accept I was body positive; at first I thought, this is not true. Then I realized the enormity of it, it had pushed me into yet another corner, this time for keeps. It quickly became a way of life: YOU AND ME, ME AND YOU. When the sun shone it became unbearable, and I didn't say anything, I had decided to be stoic, one of the fathers. This was the chance to be a grown-up. What I really felt was we should all cry, but of course I didn't, couldn't. I walked down the street in the sunlight, and everyone was so blissfully unaware. The sun is still shining.

—Derek Jarman

The last time I saw Craig, in the middle of June at his parents' home outside Chicago, he, Jane Weinstock, and I were discussing memories of when we met and how we became friends. He and I first came into contact in the late '70s at the Institute for Architecture and Urban Studies, where he was an editor of *Skyline*. I was working for an architect as an assistant. I don't think I told Craig, but as we talked, I could still see him sitting in the middle of the Institute's

main room, behind a desk, concentrating hard. He had no recollection
of me from that period. When in the next few years we'd see each
other around, he told me, I'd say hello to him and talk familiarly,
but he, he explained, was mystified as to who I was. He thought,
and even said to an acquaintance, "She's so friendly, she's going to
get hurt in a city like this." He said he felt worried about me, whoever
I was. But I have no recollection of talking to him at those times.

We became friends later, around 1983, and our friendship was
enhanced, in 1986, by his being my editor at *Art in America*. Though
we'd spent time together, working with him in his office or over
the telephone or in a bar moved our relationship into a new phase.
It was he who asked me "as a fiction writer" to contribute to the
magazine's Renoir symposium; for this I came up with a Madame
Realism piece. It was the first time that my character Madame
Realism had ever been employed as an art critic. Craig accompanied
me to Boston for the Renoir exhibition and enjoyed being part of
a subterfuge: I pretended to be listening to a docent on a museum
tape, when in fact I was recording the public's comments. He
thought that was a riot. The two of us together were not exactly
inconspicuous in the galleries—Craig at 6 feet, 7 inches had always
to bend low to suggest something to me, a mere 5 feet, 1½ inches.
We were a bit like Stan Laurel and Oliver Hardy that day, laughing,
whispering and hiding the tape recorder.

> What is at stake, then, is not only the status of narrative, but
> of representation itself.
> —Craig Owens, "The Discourse of Others:
> Feminists and Postmodernism"

I'm recollecting some moments and images I have of him, always
him in relation to me, and presenting these to you, the reader, who
may or may not have known him. Doing this brings to mind Craig's
insistence on telling us what he remembered of those early days.
Craig may have wanted us to know what his memories were, since
he knew one day he'd be gone, not able to influence directly our
and others' representations of him. And he, as much if not more

than most people, was concerned with representation in all its various articulations. I think to myself: Craig probably never thought of us as Laurel and Hardy; his experience of our day in Boston may have been extremely different from what I've written.

I believe Craig would have appreciated how his life, like a text, is available to many readings and interpretations. Probably he would have liked to have been able to control some of the interpretations, especially of his work, about which he was a severe critic. He was a critic in the broadest sense of the word—in his approach to living and to thinking, and in his capacity for delving into whatever he did with enthusiasm and immense energy. Sometimes even with a kind of mania. He was restless, not at all complacent, often impatient, and regularly horrified by the inanities and insanities of daily life. He often surprised me with responses I wouldn't have expected. It was as if he never wanted to be pinned down to one system of thought or one kind of logic. His writing, I think, demonstrates his need to examine subjects as rigorously and independently as he was able to and then, after he'd done so, to move on to other questions. Before he died he was reading Genet, Jarman and Pasolini, also Thomas Mann; he and I talked about *Death in Venice* and Genet's *Prisoner of Love*, both of which interested him enormously and gave him pleasure. Solace also, I think.

Still I wonder, and may always wonder, how he'd like to be remembered and represented. Not heroically—he'd laugh at that. One would be forgetting irony. Not melodramatically—unless, I guess, Douglas Sirk were directing. Not dramatically—unless one were Pasolini or maybe Fassbinder. Perhaps his life as an experimental narrative film by Jarman, with complexity built into the images and text. Or he might love an opera based on issues that mattered to him—homosexuality, paranoia, and fascism, concepts that he was attempting to theorize the last two years of his life. He would want the arias sung by Jessye Norman and Teresa Stratas. But could one have written a libretto and music that would make him gasp at its intelligence, its beauty and, when performed, the beauty of its execution? Wouldn't Craig have been the person to have written it?

1990

Index